PRAISE FOR JOSHUA M. FERGUSON
AND *ME, MYSELF, THEY*

"Joshua M. Ferguson's raw, extraordinary, and profoundly moving memoir provides a well needed voice for often misunderstood non-binary people. Joshua teaches us a valuable lesson about how there are no rules or limits to self-expression, and how we can look beyond the gender binary to understand the core of who we are. I was emotionally enlightened and marvel at Joshua's courage and ability to garner strength through their most painful memories. Joshua's memoir rocked me to the core while providing deep respect and understanding of those who are non-binary. It is truly inspiring to hear the story of an individual so untethered in the expression of their authentic self."
— Jazz Jennings

"Joshua M. Ferguson's *Me, Myself, They* is a necessary antidote to the impoverished modes of thinking and relating that govern our shared moment. It is a rousing call for empathy and care. It asks us to widen the terrain of gender and, in so doing, to fashion a new world. This is some of the most important work of our time, and Joshua's memoir is a beacon!"
— Billy-Ray Belcourt, author of *This Wound is a World*

"*Me, Myself, They* shows how vulnerability can be strength, how trans and non-binary people's ingenuity and creativity have carved out new paths for future generations, and how difference can—and should—be celebrated. We are all lucky that Joshua M. Ferguson has written this generous, accessible, and moving book."
— Alicia Elliott, author of *A Mind Spread Out on the Ground*

"It takes courage for gender-nonconforming people to name when the world has treated us with cruelty. I'm grateful Joshua has that courage and then some."
— Jacob Tobia, author of *Sissy: A Coming-of-Gender Story*

"For those cis folks who don't understand the trans experience, Joshua lets us into their mind. From birth to now, we see how this beautiful human found themselves. This work is important and generous and special. Thank you, Joshua, for making trans folk feel seen. May this book serve as the start of a conversation and lead to love, healing, and acceptance of our trans community."

—Gloria Calderón Kellett,
executive producer of *One Day at a Time*

"Joshua M. Ferguson's powerful and inspiring memoir, *Me, Myself, They,* is a wonderfully unique exploration of self-identity and transformation. Parents: this enlightening book is essential reading, for it will empower you to encourage the full, authentic range of your child's expression, with freedom from the confines of gender stereotyping."

—Isa Dick Hackett, producer of film and television,
and Trustee, Philip K. Dick Trust

"*Me, Myself, They* candidly and bravely shares Joshua's fascinating method for spinning trauma into gold. Buy this book. You will see yourself and love what you see."

—Jeffrey Marsh, author of *How to Be You:
Stop Trying to Be Someone Else and Start Living Your Life*

"In our slippery social moment where transgender people are by turns celebrated and reviled for their refusal to fit neatly into prescribed gender norms of girl and boy, woman and man, we need stories that illuminate fluid identity pathways. Joshua M. Ferguson brings us inside the messy, unfinished process of reclaiming new dimensions of themselves as a non-binary artist, partner, family member, scholar, and being in the world. Alive with searing details of discrimination, poignant moments of unforeseen connection, and beautiful courage, *Me, Myself, They* is a remarkable memoir that untangles the complexity of gender transformation and reminds us of the imperative to recognize who we are and deserve to become."

—Dr. Treena Orchard, Associate Professor,
School of Health Studies, Western University

Me, Myself, They

LIFE BEYOND THE BINARY

JOSHUA M. FERGUSON

ANANSI

...ua M. Ferguson

Published in Canada in 2019 and the USA in 2019 by
House of Anansi Press Inc.
www.houseofanansi.com

House of Anansi Press is committed to protecting our natural
environment. As part of our efforts, the interior of this book is printed
on paper that contains 100% post-consumer recycled fibres, is acid-
free, and is processed chlorine-free.

23 22 21 20 19   1 2 3 4 5

Library and Archives Canada Cataloguing in Publication

Title: Me, myself, they : life beyond the binary / Joshua M. Ferguson.
Names: Ferguson, Joshua M., 1982– author
Identifiers: Canadiana (print) 2018904957X | Canadiana (ebook)
20189049588
| ISBN 9781487004774(softcover) | ISBN 9781487004781 (EPUB)
| ISBN 9781487004798 (Kindle)
Subjects: LCSH: Ferguson, Joshua M., 1982- | LCSH: Gender
nonconformity.
| LCSH: Gender-nonconforming people.
Classification: LCC HQ77.9 F47 2019 | DDC 305.3—dc23[/.;'[];p

Library of Congress Control Number: 2018962108

Cover and text design: Alysia Shewchuk
Cover photo: Brendan Meadows
Typesetting: Laura Brady

 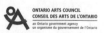

*We acknowledge for their financial support of our publishing program
the Canada Council for the Arts, the Ontario Arts Council, and the
Government of Canada.*

Printed and bound in Canada

For Florian

CONTENTS

AUTHOR'S NOTE

THIS BOOK IS MADE up of my own experiences. I do not speak for the entire trans community, or for all non-binary trans people. Nor do I have all the answers to questions about gender identity and gender expression. These pages contain my opinions. I am not the sole voice, nor am I the sole authority on non-binary gender. There are many powerful and talented trans people out there working to counter our exclusion, erasure, and invisibility. I would not be able to tell the stories in this book without the genera-tions of "transgender warriors"—a naming borrowed from groundbreaking activist and author Leslie Feinberg[1]—who have carved visible, physical, and written spaces with their bravery, insight, and talent. We are united under the banner

---

1 Leslie Feinberg (1949–2014) was known for hir novel *Stone Butch Blues* (1993) and hir non-fiction works *Trans Liberation: Beyond Pink or Blue* (1998) and *Transgender Warriors: Making History from Joan of Arc to Dennis Rodman* (1996).

of our identities. But our various perspectives contain many differences; our community is incredibly diverse.

I acknowledge the limitations and the specificities of my experiences and my perspectives in this book. One such specificity is the automatic privilege afforded to me by being white. Some of the stories told in this book are bound up in this privilege. The specificity of my stories exists, in part, because of this privilege; my voice and many of my stories would not be the same if I were a trans person of colour. So, I give you these stories while also acknowledging the importance of elevating diverse perspectives in our community, especially those of trans people of colour, including non-binary people of colour, Two Spirit people, and Indigenous trans people — voices more marginalized and silenced than my own.

I look forward to the day when an entire bookshelf of trans memoirs can exist as a testament to our rich and varied stories.

The Non-Binary Person

MOMENTS AFTER I WAS born, my mom asked the delivering physician, "What is it?"

He replied, "It's a girl!" She named me Kate in that moment before the physician said, in a curious tone, "Oh, wait…"

I like to imagine my parents' confused faces in that moment. "Oh, wait…" what? I don't blame my parents if they were confused or curious about what the doctor might say next.

And there I was, as I was supposed to be, without being told who to be, for just a few seconds. But it didn't last. The confusion passed, and soon the declarations of "It's a girl!" were replaced with — you guessed it — "It's actually a boy!"

"His name is Joshua," my parents exclaimed proudly.

And just like that, my sex was assigned, wrapped up neatly and adorned with a blue bow — and all the gender expectations that came with it.

Looking back, I'm thankful for those few seconds when I existed as the true Joshua—the Joshua that I would return to in my adulthood. The space contained in that ellipsis, those few seconds, is who I am; it was a symbolic moment, a powerful forecast of my future. Thirty years passed before I found that non-binary space again, before I found me again.

AN EVOLVING OPENNESS and awareness in discussion of gender and a growing public interest in trans lives is undeniable. The rise of high-profile trans people in the media has helped to elevate trans lives to a mainstream focus. We have become increasingly conscious of the ways in which gender dominates our existence, our identities, and our relationships from birth to death, and even beyond, lingering behind to mark our lives: "What a great *man* he was"; "What a great *woman* she was."

But what if I'm neither? My life tells a different kind of transition story. I've transformed my past to get back to who I was at birth, the person I was meant to be: the child who never felt like a boy or a girl. But this child couldn't be that person at all. This child grew without voice, presence, or agency; every dehumanizing word, push, punch, spit, threat, assault, and attack forced the essence of me deeper into the margins, and I lost myself for decades until, through trials and strength and self-examination, I was able to reconnect with that essence, beyond the trauma, and bring me back home to myself.

Me, Myself, They elevates a topic that has only recently begun to receive attention in mainstream discussions of gender: non-binary identity and expression. But the pages in this book aren't exclusively focused on my non-binary life. My non-binary trans identity is a part of me, a part of me that I lost, but I want to present the wholeness of my identity, my life, and my humanity, beyond the subject of my gender identity and how I express myself. *Me, Myself, They* is a full-circle story about how I found myself — the lost child within me — and how that made it possible for me to become the person I was meant to be. This book is about the survivor I had to become. It's about the empathy that emerged from the transformation of my trauma, and the magical alchemy, stretching out across multiple artistic pathways, that I found within myself to harness and reshape my pain and confusion into power.

Instead of organizing my narrative chronologically, from childhood to adolescence to adulthood, I've arranged the chapters thematically around different facets of my identity. My stories of the events that made me who I am today — these layers of my identity — are shared willingly, with an open heart. I want to make vital connections, from one human being to another. I believe this connection is what truly matters. I hope an understanding can be reached as you journey through my stories.

At the very beginning of our lives, we are transformed into human beings: from an "it" to a "boy" or "girl." For some, this binary sex and gender assignment takes place even before birth on the screen of an ultrasound machine that displays tiny shapes in shadow and light and reveals a girl or boy, to the delight of parents-to-be. And then this discovery is celebrated with family and friends during gender-reveal parties that carve out a baby's identity before they can even take their first breath. It happens to all of us; all infants are assigned a gender. But this script fails people who do not fit neatly into the binary. Why does gender matter so much at birth?

Our notions of gender are dependent on both culture and history. Culture makes what we assume about gender seem like an unchanging fact, something we must simply accept. However, the concept of gender is highly variable across many cultures around the world, and our relationship to it has changed over time. This context is key because we come to understand gender, and we express and present gender, from repetitive scripts that are specifically mandated in each culture. These scripts relate to our bodies (usually only two types of bodies) and how we dress them, to our gestures and mannerisms, to our language, our emotions, and our desires. For this reason, we refer to gender as a "socially constructed" concept.

Sex and *gender* are generally used interchangeably in our society to mean the same thing. At the same time that a human being is assigned a sex at birth, based almost always and exclusively on their external genitalia, they are also assigned a gender that lines up with that sex. So, for example, many people understand their gender identity (man, woman, non-binary, and so on) to describe both their *sex* and their *gender*. And if your assigned sex and gender identity line up according to societal expectations, the term that identifies you is *cisgender*—that is, if you are assigned male, you are also a man; if you are assigned female, you are also a woman. (You are welcome to visit the glossary on page 243 for a thorough discussion of some of this terminology and other language.) But while the two terms might mean the same thing for many people, *sex* and *gender* carry different meanings, highlighting their complexity.

Sex is determined by a combination of chromosomes, external and internal morphology (genitalia and reproductive organs), and hormones. Yet, physicians assign sex simply based on one part of many sex characteristics. One in every 1,500 people is born *intersex*—that is, with a variation of chromosomes, hormones, and external and internal morphology that doesn't match up with the typical definitions of male and female. In Canada, that means roughly twenty-four thousand people, or .6 percent of the population, are born intersex every year. Some intersex people identify as non-binary. Being born with sex characteristics that may not strictly align with male or female chromosomes or external and internal morphology illustrates a diversity of sex that parallels gender diversity.

In the past, I thought that the distinction between sex and gender was an important one to make—while we are born with a predetermined sex, our expressions of gender were less fixed and more fluid. But transitioning into a body that is marked by non-binary sex characteristics (what could be considered a mix of sex characteristics for my external morphology, and a mixture of hormones) has made me appreciate that sex and gender are really more similar than they are different. Both sex and gender are more fluid than they are fixed. And while conflating sex and gender makes sense for cisgender people, it also makes sense for many of us who don't neatly fit within a binary notion of bodies and identities. In other words, both sex and gender can be understood as encompassing inclusive, not exclusive, categories.

Human beings are (supposed to be) the most evolved species on the planet. So, why do we think that we are limited exclusively to a binary? Why have we rejected diversity in favour of simplicity when it comes to gender and sex? Biology in nature is complex. There are species with multiple genders (and sexes, if we accept the conflation). In *Evolution's Rainbow*, evolutionary biologist Joan Roughgarden argues that in nature there are many species that exhibit a wide spectrum of gender diversity, including many species of fish (bluegill sunfish have three sexes), kangaroos, leopard slugs, American brown and black bears, hummingbirds, and tree lizards. And scientists have reported fungi having over thirty-six thousand sexes. (The fungus world definitely sounds welcoming!) Nature is not limited by the human notion of a binary that stems from culture.

Why do human beings think that the whole picture of gender is complete with only two options? And why is this idea considered normal? Non-binary people prove, simply by existing, that what our society considers to be "normal" may not be what it seems.

Non-binary means any identity and expression that doesn't fit within the two gender and sex options presented to us at birth—that one must be a male/boy or a female/ girl. Non-binary gender identity and expression creates space for people to be who they are instead of being told who to be from the moment they are born. *Identity* is how we conceive of who we are in our mind. *Expression*, or presentation, is often linked to our identity but not always, and relates to our behaviour, mannerisms, and style of dress. Both our identity and expression are often tied to a dominant cultural script, repeated actions that are habituated as "normal."

And non-binary isn't the only identity that people use to reject the binary notion of gender. Beyond *man* and *woman*, many identities and expressions exist, such as, but not limited to, the following Western terms: *agender* (meaning people who identify without gender), *bigender* (identifying with two or more genders at the same time), *demigender* (identifying partially with more than one gender), *enby* (short form of *non-binary*), *genderfluid* (similar to *non-binary* but implying a fluidity in relation to a person's gender and sex identification), *genderqueer* (a term that is similar to but predates *non-binary*), *genderless* (similar to *agender*), *neutrois* (no gender at all), and *gender-nonconforming* (short form: *gnc*).

People who are neither male nor female have mobilized around *non-binary*—a word that seems to have emerged in North American and British vernacular around 2014—to describe gender beyond the binary. But people who identify and express themselves beyond the binary have always existed, and our existence has been marked by many terms in many languages. A multiplicity of genders beyond *man* and *woman* exist today, as they have throughout history, in cultures around the world. In Japan today, *ekkusu-jendā* (x-gender) people identify as an intermediate gender. So-called third genders in China (*yinyang ren*), Samoa

(*fa'afafine*), the Philippines (*bakla*), Thailand (*kathoey*), and
Tonga (*fakaleiti)* have been documented. In North America,
historical Indigenous cultures, particularly prior to colonization, included many genders and had specific language to
acknowledge gender beyond man and woman. Two Spirit
is an identity used today by some Indigenous people who
may not identify with binary gender; not all Two Spirit
people identify beyond the binary, and people can identify
as Two Spirit in relation to their gender or sexuality or
both. In South Asia, *hijra* commonly describes people who
identify as a third gender; the existence of *hijra* has been
acknowledged for thousands of years, and, in India, their
community received legal recognition in 2014.

But how does non-binary relate to the term *transgender*?
Is a non-binary person also transgender? Transgender—and
the terms *trans* and *trans people*—generally designates
people whose sex assigned at birth (male or female) does not
match up with their gender identity as a man or woman.
Some non-binary and gender-nonconforming people identify as trans or transgender while others don't.

But what does that mean? How do I understand my identity? What challenges do I face? What does my daily life look
like as a non-binary person? How do I engage with my body
and my sexuality? What inspires me, and what has enabled
me to find myself? And why can't I just identify with one
gender, male or female? Why can't I just be "normal"? Am
I "normal"? Are any of us "normal"? So many questions,
I know...but I found myself while trying to answer these
questions.

Non-binary: a gender identity and gender expression that isn't exclusively female/woman or male/man. Some non-binary people identify as multiple genders (for example, man and non-binary or a non-binary woman), one gender, or no gender at all. It's an identity that is open to anyone who feels included by its meaning, which may shift with time to continue to be inclusive.

The "born in the wrong body" narrative about trans people that is often reported in the media does not encapsulate my story. I was not born in the wrong body. I was born into a culture that has a narrow understanding of how bodies determine sex and gender for life.

I am neither a man nor a woman. My body and my sex are constantly shifting. As such, my transition story might be new to you. For me, transition is not a linear, one-way direction with a beginning, middle, and end. I will likely never arrive at the end of my transition. There hasn't been a death and rebirth during transition. Rather, my gender is fluid. My sexed body shifts with my gender identity and expression. So, instead of *transition*, implying an end, I prefer the term *transitioning*. I am always going to be transitioning, never fully transitioned, because being non-binary for me is about allowing myself to be free to be who I am.

You might be reading this book because you have questions about my gender, your identity, or the identity of people you know. You might be confused, curious, or even a little afraid. But fear not, you hold power while you read this book. I will always be here in these pages, in these words. I ask only one thing of you: meet me with empathy. We are all growing, learning, and trying to be who we are in the face of pervasive fear and division. We can come together through our shared humanity—our uniqueness can also be our sameness, and it can unite us.

I want to paint a horizon of hope with my story. I want us to begin to understand that human diversity is neither a weakness, a threat, nor a fiction. Our diversity is a gift, and it is an undeniable reality.

The act of storytelling is a powerful practice in many cultures around the world. It is in the act of my storytelling, both with my own stories and the stories of others, that I have come to know more about myself. Now in my thirties, after decades of confusion and fear, I have reclaimed, from my early childhood, my gender-creative self. The connections between who I am and the person I've always been are now clear to me, and I want to share this feeling of freedom with you, now situated fully in my reality.

We all remember the freedom we felt as children, the purity and innocence we felt about the world and the people around us. There is a magic in childhood. We grow up boxing ourselves in, reducing ourselves, slipping into comfortable spaces and identities to carry on with our lives, and for some of us this simply doesn't work. Being told who you are creates suffering. We can lose touch with ourselves. This leads to a painful existence.

I was always in search of something that felt lost. But the truth is that I've been there all along. I was just lost to myself. I'm ready to share me, myself, and *they*, with you.

We emerge, though always here
Renewing liminality
Eschewing rationality
Abandoning humanity's sea of fear
Swimming in fluid subjectivity free
as my self with others who are not, never, others
Unbroken from assignments
Untamed from narratives amassed from masses
Free in fluidity, eternally

ONE

The Child

I CAN RECALL ALMOST every detail of the room. The shadows holding layered depths of suffering that filled every inch. A large window overlooking a nearby park suggested something, some life, existing beyond this claustrophobic space, where I began to think that I was wrong, out of order, incomplete.

My body didn't feel sick, and yet I was being treated as though I was ill. This is the very bottom of a reservoir of trauma collected in my body, in my mind, that will never leave. There were tests, measures, questions, penetrating gazes, photographs, bloodwork. Emotions overwhelm me recalling this room. The space holds waves of sadness, confusion, and pain. Why?

Little Joshua — or, at the time, little Josh — a confused eight-year-old child, sat in this room with a large toy house. It was almost big enough to climb inside. The house was hard to ignore, beckoning me to think beyond the clinical space that I occupied. Other toys lay scattered across the floor and spilled out of boxes. It was a space of illusion, and I could feel it. A medical fix was being spun to dispel my "sickness," my foolish, childish, "gender-creative" self, and to enforce a false narrative that determined who I should be in adulthood.

Sitting across from me was Dr. Turner, a woman in her early senior years with short, curled white hair, round glasses that sat on the edge of her nose, and a slight smile. She seemed kind enough. Dr. Turner encouraged me to play while she observed my behaviour and asked questions. I had no choice but to open myself up to her "testing." During each session, I held on to a three-inch plastic toy. This toy had the exemplar "Barbie" body that was supposed to represent women, the narrow representation that we are taught at a young age to read as female: breasts, long hair, small hips, and a shapely yet slim figure. I picked this toy time and time again out of the hundreds of options in the room. I clung to this tiny plastic figure during my sessions with Dr. Turner, even as I had the feeling that I was being studied. Over the course of my visits, I began to feel like some sort of alien or monster from the cartoons that I watched on television, as though I must have something to hide. Was there something I didn't know about myself? Was there something deeply wrong about me?

I didn't realize at the time what was happening, but I was being tested because of my gender-creative expression and identity. *Gender-creative* is a term for a kind of gender nonconformity in which children can be free to explore their gender expression and identity across a spectrum of possibilities not limited to the binary, and not be told who to be. In the late 1980s, gender creativity was considered an abnormality. Testing me, the human being, the child that I was, carved a hole out of me and ripped from me the self I was born to be. Slowly, I was becoming aware of the conflict between my identity and what people thought I should be simply because of the body that I was born into.

The gender testing with Dr. Turner went on for months. I was studied like an animal in a laboratory. I became the aberration, soaking up a sense of dehumanization with every sting of the needle that took my blood, the pages and pages of questions that made up antiquated psychological tests, and ink-blot Rorschach images that were flashed in front of my face illustrating monsters for the child "monster." I worried that the world would disappear from under my feet if I gave the wrong answer, or that people might suddenly rush into the room to take me away from my parents, from my home. This process stripped away the curious and creative Joshua, it stole away a part of me, and instead I became an object of study.

My parents always switched places with me at the end of these tests. I would sit alone outside Dr. Turner's office on a cold plastic chair, feeling confused, while they received their "directions" from the doctor. I can hear my mom's muffled crying through the door. I see her worried face. I sense their desire for me to be "normal" like the son they expected, the boy named Josh they both thought they could hold on to for their entire lives.

· · ·

MY LIFE BEGAN WITH a fiction. The script was crafted. Birth came with baggage that took me almost three decades to unpack: Joshua Mark Ferguson. And then an amendment to that script was drafted by Dr. Turner. I had somehow been living outside of the acceptable terms. But there was no sickness. This was the first of many instances in my life in which the truth of others tried to shape me into something else — another person or identity that was more other people's fact than my own truth.

The tests were meant to make some sense of me, or to help my parents understand me. The more insidious aim was to correct me along the lines of a pathology, to recraft me into a "normal" child. I didn't present to my parents with an urgency for health care intervention. I was gender-creative. There was nothing wrong with me. My gender creativity was right, not wrong. It was a perfectly valid form of exploration in my childhood, something akin to the experience of most children. Gender-creative children express themselves beyond what is expected according to the gender assigned to them at birth and the behaviour, mannerisms, and play that society assumes from boys or girls.

As a gender-creative child, I played with Barbies, was obsessed with the cartoon *Jem and the Holograms*, and knew every word of Cyndi Lauper's "She Bop," which I would spin and dance to for hours on end at four years old. *Jem* was a favourite because the theme song, "Truly Outrageous," was a fierce declaration of identity. At the beginning of every episode, I would stand up and prepare myself, barely able to contain my joy when the theme song started to play. My parents watched their four-year-old "boy" become excited by a fantasy of becoming this female cartoon character who had light-purple hair and pink makeup, with all of its 1980s punk-rock flair. They could see the joy in my eyes while I danced and sang along to the show. I was undeniably happy expressing myself in ways that weren't expected of me and my gender assignment. I wanted to explore my identity through my expression, to be creative with my gender, and not wholly accept the expectations that I should like the cartoons, music, and activities that other "boys" around me were expected to like.

Though Dr. Turner's tests instilled in me a deep self-hatred, I don't blame my parents for subjecting me to them. I blame the system. I was born in the early 1980s, when all trans people were classified as having a mental illness. To be "transgender" meant that a person was sick, an idea that persists as a way to strip us of our human dignity. The only way parents could understand children who presented confusion about their gender identity or sex was through the lens of the medical system and the dominant societal understanding. The gender testing that I experienced existed in a framework of pathology that led in one direction only: towards "gender identity disorder" (as it was called in the 1980s). There was nothing in the medical lexicon that would allow for an understanding of gender identity and expression beyond "boy" and "girl."

The conceptual framework employed by physicians and specialists in medical and therapeutic fields has evolved significantly since that time. Today, trans kids don't necessarily face the same dehumanizing and objectifying methods that broke me as a child. However, many trans people are still being subjected to a process known as gender conversion therapy (also known as gender reparative therapy, or cure therapy), a regressive and transphobic practice denounced by health organizations around the world. Gender conversion therapy aims to "cure" children and adults by repressing their identity and converting them into the boy or girl identity assigned at birth. This attempted conversion of trans children still occurs despite the widely adopted health care standard for treating gender dysphoria (the current and acceptable medical definition for people experiencing emotional and psychological distress related to the sex and correlated gender assigned at birth) that simply accepts and supports trans children for who they are. Conversion forces trans kids to try to accept the gender they were assigned at birth in much the same way that the medical profession once attempted—and still does in some places in the world—to convert gays and lesbians to heterosexuality.

It was almost three decades later, while writing this book, that I realized I was a victim of the now widely and justly condemned gender conversion therapy. It is a stamp on the very essence of who I am. It is a stamp on my spirit. This "therapy" was the beginning, at age eight, of an incessant dehumanization that became a burden almost impossible to bear. A child should never be damaged by having their very identity, individuality, ripped from them. This wound will be with me forever. A monster of hate and shame took its painful shape within me.

•   •   •

THERE ARE GAPING HOLES in the fabric of my childhood memories. The pervasive testing, the wounds that were made by breaking me as a child, and the trauma that ensued account for these failures. They are suspicious blanks that are inaccessible. Perhaps these blockages save me from pain and enable me to move forward with my life. These memories may never be found. They've vanished to help me survive. It disturbs me. Some of the smells, colours, emotions, and words that make up our many moments and that others seem to be able to recollect in vivid details are gone. Much of my life seems to be gone, tucked away, and trauma has taken its place.

Yes, I was born into an incorrect sex assignment and correlated gender identity. I was born into a gender already manufactured. But I was born from two very beautiful people whose love for me transcended all the confusion, even their own. Two people who always accepted me, despite trying to help me in the damaging way they thought best. These two people, Mark and Kimberly, followed their dreams, created a beautiful family, and did their best as parents in spite of their own challenging histories.

My father's favourite photograph of himself shows him in a kilt, wearing all the Scottish accessories you can imagine, and holding a high-quality replica of the sword from *Braveheart*. My dad studied biology at McGill University and met my mom, Kimberly, while they were both at university in Montreal. He was a fish and wildlife biologist with the Ministry of Natural Resources in Ontario. Later, he worked for the Department of Fisheries and Oceans Canada. None of my friends' parents did anything nearly so interesting, and the uniqueness of his work life intrigued me. I was proud to have a father who was an expert in his field. His professional passion to protect fish and wildlife habitats influenced how I was raised, and I spent much of my time in the outdoors. He taught me to notice and respect non-human sentient beings. I gained an appreciation for the sensitive systems at play in habitats, and how human beings have endangered nature and sentient life. Although he worked within a system of government enacting policy and law, he was propelled by a passion in his work as a biologist that inspired me to care deeply about enacting change, to use knowledge and voice in action to make a difference. Both of my parents, each in their own way, are caretakers of nature, the land, and people.

My father is a sensitive man, well-read and well-educated, with a sharp intellect, one that was frequently challenged by me. His background in science meant that we had some heated debates when I began to engage with philosophical thought, but it was healthy to grow up with a parent who challenged me intellectually. During my childhood and adolescence, it felt like a constant struggle with my dad, and not simply because I was gender-creative. As a child, I was challenging, a bit wild, sensitive, emotional, and curious. My parents have often said over the course of my life that I was "difficult," and that hasn't always been entirely fair. I think it's easy for parents to label a child "difficult" without ever wanting to understand the source of the difficulty.

I know that I overwhelmed my dad with being a "difficult" kid. I get that it wasn't easy to raise a kid who expressed their gender beyond what was expected of me and said things like "I think God made a mistake with my body." I know that it couldn't have been easy on either of my parents. I tested them, pushed them, disobeyed them, and made them worry about me. I get it. But being told you are a "difficult" child places sole responsibility for the behaviour directly on you, rather than looking at the whole family structure and how it contributes to why the child is difficult in the first place. Kids soak up everything; we don't give them enough credit for how aware they are, starting at a very young age.

I was my parents' first child, born to them in their mid-twenties, and we lived in a small apartment in Brantford for the first year of my life. Apparently, I cried so loud at night that even the neighbours complained, and my parents had to pad the bottom of the door to my room with towels to get a little rest. I'm not a parent, so I wouldn't know exactly how exhausting it is to have children. And I've never been sure if my parents calling me "difficult" was related to my gender-creativity and all the social pressures they must have faced because of it, or if I was just a child who challenged my parents as their first-born.

I know most parents need space from their children; they need time to themselves. But I was always deeply aware of my dad's need to distance himself, and it bothered me. There were times when he lost his patience with me as I frequently questioned the order of things and asserted myself. I felt as though he had to shut himself down to get away from his "difficult" child. Their bedroom door would close, and the house would go dark sometimes. I'm not sure he ever understood how much this distancing isolated me even more.

Nevertheless, he never failed to accept me. I wasn't forced away from my home because of my queer sexuality or gender nonconformity. And, thanks in part to a cultural shift that saw a greater social acceptance of LGBTQ people in the early 2000s and led to a broader understanding, both of my parents embraced my difference and let go of the guilt they had carried for trying to tame a child like me. My dad has always loved me. He loves me for who I am, including my non-binary identity, even though it brought him a great deal of worry and it wasn't always easy.

My mom, Kimberly, was born and raised in York, Pennsylvania, and her family had deep roots in the city. She was a beautiful woman from a young age, and her beauty leaves an impression on everyone she meets. She has sharp, deep-green eyes with yellow rings around the pupils that look like the brightest sun coming out to greet you from deep within the forests of her soul. And, her smile. Her smile is a circle of happiness that carries forth her bellowing laugh, which always makes me feel love. She's a free spirit with a deep heart-well.

In her professional life, my mom was a caretaker, not unlike my dad. But instead of caring for nature and wildlife, she channelled her kindness and compassion into taking care of people. She became a registered nurse in her early twenties working in emergency rooms, sometimes in rural areas, and so she was frequently confronted with suffering and mortality. She transitioned to serving in a forensic ward as a mental health nurse when I was a child. I have always been proud of her and impressed by her ability to treat mentally ill people. She is nurturing but she is also tough when she needs to be.

My mother is a deeply resilient and powerful woman. She survived both sexual abuse and violence in her childhood home, and she struggled for decades with undiagnosed mental illness. When I was a young adult, she was diagnosed with bipolar disorder. I was the first of her three children, and her feminine beauty comforted me in a house full of masculine energy, and it somehow made me feel less alone. I can see myself in her eyes and her face, reflecting parts of me, reminding me of where I came from. She always saw me, saw herself within me, but she worried deeply about me, especially when I was young. Perhaps she worried about the parts of her that she had to hide to survive the suffering of her own upbringing. A part of me — the free soul aching to fly — might have scared her because it reminded her painfully of her own need to conform to survive in a different time, in a different generation.

During my adolescent years, my parents' marriage began to break down. My parents were always apologizing to me, while at the same time calling me "special" for my free spirit, for my academic accomplishments at an early age, and for my expressive personality. Since I was both "special" and "difficult," I grew up feeling like both a gift and a burden to my family.

My parents wrote me letters sporadically over the years, mostly at Christmastime, from the time when I was about six. I'd always wondered why they wrote out their feelings rather than communicating verbally, so I asked them while reflecting for this book. They wanted me to have a record, they said, a memory of my childhood years and how our relationship evolved. The letters—they wrote to my brothers, as well—were a gift to us. Each letter was meant to capture a particular moment in the life of our family. In reality, the conflicting perspective on my "special" and "difficult" personality was framed within these letters. I would read them over and over again. And often I would tear them up whenever I faced challenges with my parents. Destroying their words felt empowering, an outlet for my frustration with their frustration, and it made me feel more in control of their criticism. The tears in these letters, now yellowed by the ageing tape keeping them together, represent a tension I faced at home, too.

When I was nine, my mom wrote, "You have always enjoyed playing with girls' toys and playing with girls and I know that sometimes you wish you were a girl. That's OK. Josh, you can't change your feelings." Then, when I was sixteen, after coming out to them as gay at the time, she writes, "It's not always easy being different. I bet that it's really hard to be you most of the time—'the real Josh.'" The fact that my mom recognized me by trying to help me see my intrinsic self at times in my life when I started to lose touch with that shows how much she loved me and cared about my own truth. These letters were opened with anticipation and excitement whenever we would receive them. They embodied the unspoken feelings of my parents, of our family at challenging times when, depleted by the pressures of parenting and professional demands, they were not always able to discuss everything out in the open. The letters were reflective and motivational. Now, reading them again, I understand that they were writing to themselves as much as they were writing to me and my brothers.

My dad's letters advise me to "surround myself with great people" and ask me to "understand and be patient with me as sometimes I try to rush you into acting your age or be a certain way." Dad made an effort to tell me I was special, but he also admitted to wanting to control who I was through disciplining me, expecting me to behave with a maturity beyond my age or be more responsible as the eldest child in the family.

A consistent theme in these letters is apology. They are sorry for yelling, being mad at me, "losing my temper," "crossing the line." These behaviours established a pattern in my relationships with them for years to come. And my parents' apologies have spilled into my relationships with others, where I feel cautious about people wanting to con trol me or encouraging me to be more like who they want me to be instead of simply being myself. They try to help me by telling me how to be someone who I'm not. I see through these gestures. People want me to be more similar to them to ease their discomfort.

MY PARENTS SUBMITTED ME to the testing because they had questions about my identity and how best to support me. They were trying to help me. They had no idea that the type of testing Dr. Turner performed would be damaging. I was born at a time when most people didn't understand what transgender meant, or know that trans people even existed. I was telling people at the young age of seven that God had made a mistake, that I was a girl living inside a boy's body, because language didn't exist to think about myself as something other than a girl or a boy. I would meet someone with my parents, and a proclamation would soon follow about my gender, to their embarrassment: "Oh, God made a mistake, you know? He really meant to make me a girl!"

I can remember feeling like a freak, like there was something seriously wrong with me whenever I saw my parents embarrassed in social situations. I'm sure they dismissed my declarations by saying that I was just confused: "You know how children are. Josh is a very creative child. This is just a phase. He'll get over it." I know that I told people God had made a mistake and that I was meant to be a girl because I could see only two options for gender: I could be a boy or I could be a girl, there was nothing else. Why *wouldn't* my parents seek help if I was saying this consistently at age seven?

I didn't learn about Dr. Turner's diagnosis until I was in my thirties, recalling pain and trauma from the experience, and I finally asked my parents what had happened. They told me that Dr. Turner had diagnosed me as a "cross-dresser," noting that I would always want to dress in "women's clothing" unless corrective measures were enacted to fix, or convert, my gender confusion back into the identity of a boy. She told my parents that they should enrol me in boys' sports, that my dad should spend more time with me, and that they should encourage me to play with boys my age.

At that time, the only term for trans people used in medical discourse was *transsexual*, which described people who transition to match their gender identity often opposite to sex assigned at birth. Non-binary expression was understood back then only as a form of "cross-dressing"; Dr. Turner and her colleagues simply could not see anything beyond the binary.

Still, it was shocking to discover that Dr. Turner had instructed my parents to "fix" me using gender corrective measures that would help me be more like a "normal" boy. Otherwise, she warned, our family would continue to face "issues" and "problems" with my gender identity and the way I expressed myself. What damaged me for so long was that her testing had a goal to correct my identity, to convert me into a "normal" boy. But, I wasn't a boy and I wasn't a "cross-dresser." I honestly can't say how successful she was, or speak to what measures she enacted to achieve her goal of "curing" my gender-creative self. I just know how the trauma has haunted me from that time, initiating a split of self that caused a dangerous and destructive form of self-hatred and lack of self-worth. Thankfully, my parents didn't follow the corrective measures she recommended. They didn't entirely believe that Dr. Turner's diagnosis was accurate, and instead chose to see me as I was. It's an understatement to say that I'm thankful for their decision to reject Dr. Turner's instructions to convert me into a "normal" boy. I'm not sure that I would have survived if they had forced me to be a certain way.

At my request, they enrolled me in ballet and local theatre and they didn't object to the fact that my best friends

were all girls, Kristin in particular, who was my best friend
in elementary school and with whom I felt like I could be
myself, the gender-creative expressive weird kid. And I did
play some sports as a child—baseball, basketball, soccer,
and tennis. The understanding seemed to be that I would
benefit from the exertion of my physical body with other
bodies that appeared like mine, playing with "other" boys,
as if sweating it out on the field would somehow begin
to reshape me into the boy they had imagined when they
named me Josh. But even when I was playing with other
boys, I still didn't feel like I belonged. I can remember
one night, while driving home from a basketball game,
my mom saying to me, "The mother sitting next to me
at the game tonight asked me if you were a boy or a girl."
Embarrassed, I asked why this woman would say that.
Mom smiled and looked at me. "I told her you are a boy,
but that you are pretty for a boy. She said you had a very
soft face." I responded with a smile and turned my gaze
to the blackness outside the car window. If a person who
knew nothing about me thought I was a girl, then why was
I trying to hide my truth by playing sports with the boys? It
was all so confusing, as I struggled to make sense of other
people's thoughts and feelings about me. They wanted me
to be a boy, the one they called Josh, while I struggled to
hold on to the gender-creative child, the Joshua that I knew
was inside me.

· · ·

AS THE YEARS PASSED, the medical interventions continued. I can't count the number of general physicians, psychologists, psychiatrists, and counsellors that I saw during my childhood and adolescence. I can't remember all of them, but I know there were at least a dozen people who examined me, mostly related to my gender identity disorder (more accurately called gender dysphoria now) and depression as a child. Therapy is necessary for some people, and I am grateful for the therapy now in my adult life, but being medically examined and dissected by others at a young age was traumatic and caused me to lose parts of myself.

And it turns out there was never anything wrong with me, or with other trans people. Gender dysphoria is no longer classified as a mental disorder in the current *Diagnostic and Statistical Manual of Mental Disorders-5 (DSM-5)*. Gender dysphoria is a distress, not a disorder or a disease. It is diagnosed when a person cannot achieve an alignment between the gender identity that they think and feel is who they truly are and the assigned-sexed body that they were born into. And much of this distress comes from the overwhelming pressure arising from the media and our culture about sex and gender. Part of my own distress comes from the social expectations people have about my identity and my body and the way these expectations are enforced upon me, sometimes in violent and dehumanizing ways.

Many people struggle to make sense of this distress from an early age. And medical professionals are only now beginning to understand that trans kids are diverse. Some kids are binary-identified trans girls and trans boys, while others are gender-creative, gender-nonconforming, or identify with a non-binary or gender-fluid identity. The immense pressure from cultural scripts—from our families, teachers, friends, and the media—makes it impossible for some of us to truly understand who we are, our identity, particularly when we are children. We are inundated, from a very young age, with cultural messages that focus on the gender binary. The binary separation of boys from girls splits us into only two possible ways of being. Instead of just being who we are, we are pushed to fit into the mould of boys' or girls' clothes, toys, washrooms, sports, careers, classes, language, behaviour, bodies, hairstyles, clothing, music—the list is endless.

It's overwhelming for some children, maybe all children, to be flooded with the either-or enforced gendered subjectivity. It isn't just trans kids who are adversely affected by the binary.

There is nothing natural about the culture that has been created around dividing people into one or the other gender. In fact, we do this with everything. It's easier for some people to understand life if we separate everything into either-or. It's easy to count the masses, categorize and control people, if we are divided into two.

Culture is far from a natural order, and gender is a cultural construct. It doesn't exist without us bringing it into existence through language, behaviour, repeated actions, and scripts. The way we think about gender today is different from a few decades ago, and it will change again. But we are, in part, stuck now in our current cultural understanding, which we project even into the future in speculative fiction, television, and film, presenting an unrealistic binary-based version of sex and gender as if the current model of binary sex and gender would even apply a hundred or two hundred years from now.

Joshua (my gender-creative self) turned into Josh (the identity that was determined for me) and the "male" sex assignment controlled the way people referred to me, the way people thought about me, and eventually how I started to understand myself. I was assigned a "male" sex at birth based on . . . what, exactly? Think about this for a moment. We allow our physical anatomy, particularly what is on the surface of our bodies, to dictate the way we identify with our sex, gender, and even sexuality throughout our life. Our genitalia literally places us under a certain set of medical, sexual, relationship, marriage, and behavioural terms that we never get to choose in the first place. Rarely do we stop to question why our external genitalia should matter so much for our identity. The physician makes a snap judgement based on a quick glance and then our identity is stamped by the script meant to keep us contained and easily counted as human beings. The script of "there are only two sexes" establishes itself as fact and we become acceptable babies on either side of the binary.

And just as my assigned male sex made me a boy, my sexuality was assumed to be heterosexual, because this is considered the default — any other identity for sexuality has to be declared. Heteronormativity, a term to describe the automatic assumption that people are heterosexual, also establishes itself as an unquestioned fact. It's overwhelming to consider the baggage that this creates for everyone, not just for trans people.

I think about little Joshua. The Joshua who danced and sang so freely to the *Jem* theme song, Cyndi Lauper's "She Bop" and "Girls Just Want to Have Fun," and Madonna's "Vogue" and "Express Yourself." I explored who I was by dressing up in a variety of clothing to express my fluid gender identity. With my two brothers, Adam and James, I would create fantastical characters—one called Power Girl stands out—and we would put on performances for my parents inspired by the props and costumes we played with. James, nicknamed "Peanut" by my parents, is four years younger than me. His inquisitive and playful mind was apparent to me at a young age. Both brothers were open to expressing our expressive selves at this age.

It was a safe time from the ages of four to eight. It was a time when my gender expression was treated as a part of my free child spirit instead of a problem. I used to love spinning around and around while dancing with my brothers, the space around me blurring into a beautiful picture of complexity to match how I was feeling. The world was too slow to catch up to my spinning. I was existing in my own space, spinning around in a circle, feeling the rush of my energy in an in-between space where I felt free. Then I had to stop the spinning, snap back to reality and what awaited me in the years ahead. I was me back then. My spirit was able to breathe before the medical intervention that destroyed a piece of me.

I was lost within myself, in the layers of examination, the projected confusion from my parents, friends, teachers, and people in the community, simply for being different. Why couldn't I just exist as I was? I got lost in the darkness;

each test dimmed the light of my spirit more and more. In the lines of others' scripts and stories, not my own, I was forced to accept a false narrative, one that made sense for others but not for me.

I became so tired of being the Josh that was created for me at birth. It is exhausting to be someone else, an identity that isn't your own. Saying "Josh," hearing "Josh," seeing Josh, and accepting he/him/his pronouns made me feel foreign to my own self. I had to excavate myself out of the foundation of being that was built for me without my say.

TWO

The Fluidity

THE EMERGENCE OF THE WORD *non-binary* to describe gender identity and gender expression happened relatively recently. It grew out of a space of reclamation, of carving out a place for our recognition from the shadows of our erasure. We had to actualize our identity within language. *Non-binary* has now become part of our lexicon.

I found a home in the word *non-binary* because it welcomed my fluid gender. I feel safe with the meaning of *non-binary*, a word that signals space to allow for change and growth. Non-binary is, for me, about fluidity. Comfort is important when it comes to our identities. Yet my gender identity and gender expression haven't always been the same, and they will no doubt change multiple times throughout my life. *Non-binary*'s promise exists in its potential to be an inclusive term, to offer a safe home for those of us who shift identities throughout our lives. My gender, and the way that I express myself, isn't static, but my identity as non-binary can be fixed throughout my life. Although, I'm not entirely sure that my identity will remain fixed. This might be confusing. Actually, I'm sure it's all a bit confusing!

Let me first explain what I mean by feeling certain about being non-binary while still having a fluid gender and a gender expression that shifts with time. I don't think that I was born with a non-binary identity. You are likely familiar with the "born this way" narrative that's been used by the LGBTQ community to encourage acceptance and tolerance when it comes to our human rights and equal rights. Well, it's become an almost immutable narrative to explain how trans identity works. The "born this way" story emphasizes that trans people have always been trans, because we are born with our identities in the first place. For example, according to this concept, most trans women and trans men are born with a gender identity as either a man or a woman, but this gender identity doesn't always match their sex assigned at birth. And some non-binary people feel that they were born non-binary. This is the truth for much of our community, and it is perfectly valid.

My feeling is different. I wasn't born with an awareness of my gender identity. You know that I was assigned a "male" sex at birth; however, this was not the sex that I identified with, and the gender identity of "boy" or "man" that goes along with an assigned male sex felt completely false to me. I wasn't truly born with a gender identity, because gender is self-determined. The "born this way" narrative is necessary to challenge the less acceptable view that we can simply choose our own identities. I know that it's helpful to suggest that all trans people are born with our gender identity because then it isn't a choice, and acceptance should necessarily follow. But does this really work for all of us? If we are all born with a gender identity, then how do some of us change this identity throughout our lifetimes? Acceptance shouldn't be contingent on our identities remaining static and immutable throughout our lives.

It is in the act of coming out that we declare our identity, one that was there from birth and usually remains the same throughout our lives. But I think we can come out multiple times, because change is a part of what makes us human. In fact, I have to constantly come out so that people won't use incorrect pronouns to refer to me. I wish that, when I met people, I wouldn't have to assert my gender identity over and over again to avoid discomfort and embarrassment.

LET'S HAVE THAT TALK about pronouns. They seem to be one of the aspects of trans identity that cisgender people, or non-trans people, struggle with most. People are curious about pronouns. But there is also stress related to using the correct ones, a fear or panic that cis, and even some trans people, have when it comes to referring to us. We all operate under what we like to think is an unchanging and stable language that informs the way we speak about one another. The two available pronouns that we are conditioned to use from a very young age — he and she — represent one of the most powerful and pervasive components of language. And now that gender-neutral pronouns (particularly they/them/

their) have become part of our vernacular for people who identify beyond the binary, I want to calm some fears based on my own experience.

Pronouns are of vital importance to trans people because they are one of the primary agents of autonomy and social recognition that we have. Some trans people, rightfully so, become angry and offended by people who fail to use their pronouns when referring to them. Language for trans people can sometimes be violent—enforced upon us as our reality. The failure to use a person's pronouns, or repeated misuse of pronouns, is called *misgendering*. And if the person doing the misgendering is intentionally enacting harm and harassing a trans person by using incorrect pronouns to insist that they adhere to their sex and gender assigned at birth, this could be classified as a form of transphobic violence enacted on trans people.

To be clear, if a person makes an honest mistake, and even continues to make mistakes but unintentionally and with full regret, then I wouldn't consider this to be violent (though it can amount to laziness and disrespect). However, the deliberate refusal to acknowledge a trans person's pronouns amounts to an outright rejection of their gender identity, which is their own. No one should be able to control another person's identity. For me, it can be quite painful to consistently hear he/him/his when my pronouns are they/them/their.

Florian, my husband, took a couple of years to get into the habit of using my correct pronouns. Before I started coming out as non-binary, he habitually referred to me using he/him/his, for more than eight years. When I first came out as non-binary in 2015 and asked for they/them/their pronouns, these were not being used to the extent they are now, and he needed time to adjust to this new paradigm shift in his language. His mistakes were never malicious.

My family members have been a bit slower to adjust to the reality of my identity. It's taking them much longer to use they/them/their, and when they slip back into old habits and say he/him/his, frankly, it kind of hurts. Cis people might find it difficult to understand the pain that trans people feel when we are misgendered by our family and friends even though we have afforded them time to adapt. This pain could be avoided if cis people would do the work to use pronouns for trans people in all conversations, not just when they're around us, because then new habits would be formed. I practised patience with my family and friends for the first year or so, but I have made explicit note of my pronouns for almost four years now, so . . . what's the problem?

I think part of the issue is that some people get too caught up in themselves when they make mistakes with pronouns. They tend to forget the person in front of them who is being invalidated by the language that is used. I've experienced it many times. A person's ego gets wound up in the act of trying to use proper pronouns (or not trying at all), they make a mistake, and feel a sense of guilt. The person who used incorrect pronouns apologizes and feels bad, makes a point of saying how accepting they are, internalizes it, and the focus shifts from the actual trans person to the person who made the mistake. Instead, practising

sensitivity about the trans person being spoken of, a con-
sciousness of that person's identity, should be the focus.

Everyone makes mistakes sometimes when it comes
to pronouns. There are even times when I make honest
mistakes when referring to other trans people. I genuinely
believe, though, that many people who make mistakes do
not mean them. It's important to recode and rethink our
language to recognize trans people, but this won't happen
if we push away people who are not meaning to do harm.
We have to afford people time to work their way out of the
language that has become habitual. We can't isolate others
to make our own isolation feel better.

Consider that we aren't all born with our identities;
some of us continue to evolve, and accept the flow of our
lives and what feels truthful to us throughout our diverse
experiences. If we accept the notion that gender identity is
fluid rather than static, then we can change how we think
about one another as infinitely evolving human beings.
I have already experienced multiple genders and gender
expressions during my life, some of which I express for just
a short period of time. I wasn't ever completely and fully a
boy or a man. I was, and am, something else entirely.

I want to play with my identity. I think of it as creative,
not controlled—free and floating in a sea of imaginative
personas. I want to dislocate myself from the habitual
imperative of fixed gender identity. I want to be, and I am,
hybrid, multiple—part man, part woman, part something
else—beyond what simple language can capture.

I wish that my body could be as fluid as my identity. I
would love to change my body daily to connect with my

shifting feelings, never transitioning in a permanent way but in ways that allow me to make subtle shifts to a more hybrid embodiment of my genders. Gender dysphoria happens for me when these changes are impossible or cannot happen fast enough.

People try to correct me constantly. "What *is* Joshua?" "How do I refer to Joshua?" "What is *it*?" "Is *it* a he or a she?" Most days, I feel like an alien, like I'm from another world or planet. It would be so much easier for everyone else if I just stuck with a stable gender identity and said that I was born with it. But that isn't my truth. I prefer to be complex. And sometimes—*sometimes*—the curiosity or the desire to figure me out is welcome. But not always. I am Joshua the alien for many people. I come across people in my daily professional life—people who are creative, sensitive, and artistic—and they want to understand me. They don't want to be ignorant. I can see the need to understand in their eyes. They make mistakes and misgender me; they ask intrusive questions designed to make them feel better about who I am. I want to be open and available for them to learn from. I want to be willing to be discovered and to be explored. But sometimes it's just too much. It can be absolutely exhausting to always be open to people in this way. Most people find security within their identities because they are intelligible, stable, and follow the cultural logic of the gender binary. (The concept of *gender intelligibility* was coined by the philosopher Judith Butler.) People find commonality in these similarities. Who wants to feel excluded? We all want to feel welcome to some degree. Yet I invoke curiosity and insecurity in others. And I often find that the people who most need to ask questions, but don't, never arrive at the place of understanding. A reticence to ask questions can also mask transphobic hostility because some people may never want to understand. The people who are mindful about probing, yet want to understand, are the people who I want to have conversations with, because their reticence to ask questions can come from compassion. I want to have conversations about my identity with people who are compassionate. On an empathetic level, I always want to welcome this curiosity if it's coming from a place of compassion.

It's easier to exist in this writing than it is to stand in front of you. The drive to discover happens without the need for me to be involved in every interaction. I wonder about the realization of my non-binary identity, and how much of my path to discovering how to explain my fluid identity relates to other people's need to *know* me. Even if I explain my non-binary identity, there are people who will still try to *figure me out*. It isn't enough for them, they want to know it all, or to think that they could know it all. There must be more, or there must be a way to explain it in "rational" terms.

Consider the questions and the contradictions that arise from this discussion. We don't need to know everything to accept someone who is different from us. This drive to know everything can force us to think of everyone as either one or the other, familiar or unfamiliar, categorizable, instead of accepting that some people might be something altogether different from what we can imagine. The confusion initiates the questions and the quest to know, or to get to know, what non-binary really means for me and what it can mean for you.

I came out to Florian and my family almost four years ago as transgender, and then another coming out happened, about a year later, when I found the language of non-binary during the final stage of the research and writing of my doctoral dissertation. I discovered myself in my academic work and then came out as non-binary. I felt an immediate sense of relief when I was able to say "non-binary" out loud. It is odd to say that I "came out" because I know that my fluid gender could make me come out again and again every time it shifts throughout my life. This coming out happens in a language altogether different from what can be articulated on a verbal level. The language of coming out with the body, of coming out without words but with a fluid gender, is a new concept for many because we often rely on the vocal act of coming out to stabilize, and to secure, our identities.

There are multiple layers to coming out for me, which are certainly beyond the "born this way" narrative. I know that coming out as non-binary won't be the final time that I come out with an identity in my lifetime, but perhaps it will be the last time that such an identity is articulated with words constructed to make sense of me. I think it's easier to explain to some people in my family that I was born non-binary, but it wouldn't be truthful. There would be less opposition if I could lean on being "born that way," but it just doesn't feel right to me. The idea of being born a specific way or in a static and immutable identity seems more about appeasing the other person than about acknowledging who I am. It feels like an effort to make the other person comfortable instead of myself.

There are no rules about non-binary identity. But it also isn't about choosing frivolously from one day to the next. My experience with gender matches my feeling and the way that my self exists on and inside my body. So, saying that there are days when I still feel partly like a man or a woman doesn't disqualify me from my non-binary identity. A non-binary person could still identify as a woman and be non-binary. There are no limits to how we experience our complex self and communicate it to others. Non-binary is about being fluid.

The necessity to maintain a stable gender identity can be illusory. This need to always be the same can be about control and about comfort. It isn't always the most comfortable feeling to shift back to feeling like a man when the script of male/boy/man was enforced on my life at such an early age, but I would be lying to myself if I said that this identity wasn't still a part of my life, or wasn't a part of my life at one point. The false identities constructed for me at birth are still within me, still with me on this journey. The story of my life will always hold space for the time when I accepted the identity of a boy or a man because there was no other way or choice that I could realize at that time. I can still remember who I was when I entered puberty, and I still see that boy in the mirror looking back at me with sadness. I see that boy, growing facial hair, seeing through the reflection as if the mirror didn't hold the entire truth.

. . .

WE HAVE SIMPLIFIED GENDER to understand it and to control it in our lives. We want to try to understand it all.
Our gender is a predominant part of our life, so stability is
security and safety. But why are people transphobic? Why
do people get so angry about the thought of gender beyond
the two options we're presented with early on in life and
that are reinforced over and over throughout our lives?

I am convinced that we don't see the whole picture of
gender with "men" and "women." We need to excavate the
truth. We need to highlight the complexity of gender and
move away from oversimplifications that do damage to
ourselves and to our children, who grow up in a world full
of possibilities but lack the freedom to be who they want
to be. The absence of this freedom can bring about severe
consequences, pain, and suffering. I know this well.

THREE

The Survivor

HIS FIST SMASHES THROUGH the car window. A crimson mist paints the air, delivering his presence closer. I look down at my hands speckled with blood, not my own. My eyes shut. I feel the world closing in on me. I find the strength to glance quickly at the cellphone in my hand, just as a haze overwhelms me and my head hits the back of the seat. I feel the force of yet another blow to my face. The screaming, the shouting, and the pain all directed at me like an arrow meant to pierce my essence. I am inside a horror film. I have become the central character of some sick and twisted plot. I need to get out, or there won't be anything left of me. I will be no more.

I try to dial 911 on the small Nokia phone, but he notices. He screams: "What do you think you're doing, faggot?!" The phone is slapped from my hands.

I am alone, trapped in the passenger seat of my mom's car, a gold Saturn sedan, tilted at a sixty-degree angle and stuck in a ditch. Somewhere between life and death, I am caught and captive for the physical assault from a stranger that won't stop. He is now in the vehicle with me, this monster painted with his own blood, the flesh ripped off his knuckles after he smashed the driver's side window to get inside. He hits me again, harder this time, and it almost knocks me unconscious. The doors are locked and I can't get out. I can't even control my limbs. The fear overwhelms me and exhaustion sets in. The attacker's hateful words are partly drowned out by my panic.

Then, inside a moment where I almost lost it, where everything almost slipped away from me, I find something. I find my survivor's spirit deep within, tucked away inside the chrysalis created by the pain and suffering from my adolescence. I feel a sudden strength. My vision clears and my mind sharpens. I summon an energetic barrier between myself and my attacker, between me and this demonic monster.

I reach out to the passenger door, find the button to unlock it, and push the door open with every bit of force still left within me, summoning everything that I can possibly gather because, I know, this is the decisive moment of my life, for my life. I look around quickly to plan my escape route, glancing at the cold, dark road, over railroad tracks, and into a small shopping centre with a Tim Hortons, less than half a mile away. Time is not on my side right now. I feel frozen in this moment. It's at least two in the morning: will the coffee shop even be open?

I don't have time to consider these questions. I must escape now, or get dragged back into the blood, spit, and fear. I scramble out of this car soaked with his rage and climb out of the ditch. I can hear him screaming behind me. I see two other people on the road, likely his friends, and I know right away that they are going to try to stop me. I clutch my heart and for a moment it feels like I'm holding the muscle in my hand. I take a second to summon my last reserves of energy and spirit. And then I run.

I run on the winds of the pain and suffering. I run with the violence that I have faced throughout my life, everything that prepared me for this attack. I run with each utterance of *faggot, queer, fairy, freak, trash* that was said to me countless times. I run with the feeling of the spit that hit my face, my body, and the many pushes and shoves and punches. I run with each feeling of threat to my life. I run with the sound of this monster's taunting laughter and ridicule pushing my feet and my arms forward, propelling me. I run with these newfound wings. I am a survivor, and this won't end me. I run past two other people, down the road, over the train tracks, and into the Tim Hortons. It's still open — thank the goddess.

But I'm not safe yet. There are two employees behind the counter, and I scream, with every ounce of breath in my body, begging them to lock the doors. I try to get the words out to explain that someone has just attacked me, that I have barely escaped with my life. I immediately realize that this must appear like a nightmarish joke to them.

While the employees lock the doors I dial 911 and collapse against the wall, sinking to the floor in a state of complete exhaustion. In this coffee shop, brightly lit, I look down at my shaking hands. There is so much blood. It's all over my hands and clothes. Is it all mine? No, it's also his blood. I can feel it intruding on my soul, yet it is a sign of my triumph. This monster left me with his blood as a reminder of his weakness. He bled and he was human, not some invincible creature trying to end me. He was not invulnerable, and he would not win. His fear would not take me.

THE POLICE NEVER CAUGHT the man who attacked me that day. The monster eluded the law, and it's an injustice. He can live his life without ever facing the consequences of almost ending mine. It's a true horror story, but one in which the marginalized queer and trans person finds safety. The trans person survived.

My attack was classified by the police as a hate crime. I felt the detectives didn't take the investigation seriously because of my queer identity and my feminine gender expression. Extensive evidence was present at the scene, but the attacker and his friends were never found. The investigation wasn't handled properly. I had to reach out to the investigative team to receive updates, and they only met with me once after the attack. The attack happened in front of a house in a neighbourhood. People lived just twenty feet from the ditch. Were they watching while it was happening? Were they frozen into apathy? I've always hoped that they were fast asleep. It would sicken me to know that they had watched frozen in fear that night, or coldly immune to the inhumanity that they witnessed, and so I tell myself that they were asleep in their beds.

The three people had followed me that night from a gay bar in nearby Kingston, Ontario. I dropped someone off, an acquaintance, on my way home, and I was driving on a back road when their car appeared out of the darkness and started to follow mine, bright lights close enough to blind me. I can still feel the sick twist in my stomach when I realized that they wouldn't stop following me, that I had become their prey. I knew from that moment that this would be an event that would forever change me.

But I refused to be prey. I summoned all of the pain and suffering in my life: the abuse from my classmates in grade school, the bullies that tormented me in high school, the teachers and principals who looked the other way and wouldn't help, the friends who turned their backs on me, the sexual assaults. I channelled it all into saving myself that day. It was all preparation. I was now a survivor in my early twenties. The nightmare that had been my adolescent life was now my weapon, my armour, and my spells, reworked in my dreams, where I wielded superpowers to fend off that monster invading my reality.

MY FEMININE GENDER EXPRESSION has always evoked fear in others. I used to think that coming out as gay at age fourteen in the small town of Napanee, Ontario, was the cause of my being bullied, the reason for the harassment. Now I realize that the thing that incited the most fear in others, the most insecurity and the intense need to destroy me, was my gender expression. The bullies that entered my life at age fourteen, when I finally decided to express my gender

openly in high school, targeted me mostly because of how I
presented myself. People who are assigned male at birth but
who present feminine are either seen as betraying some sort
of unspoken order of patriarchy, or they are automatically
labelled gay, and this presumed sexuality incites insecurity
and perhaps unwelcome thoughts and feelings in others.

I had, of course, experienced bullying in elementary
school, and I had been haunted by the dehumanizing feelings instilled in me by Dr. Turner's gender conversion therapy since the age of eight. During elementary school I felt
like an outcast. Assuming the female roles from popular
cartoons in the games we would play in the schoolyard
(like April from *Teenage Mutant Ninja Turtles* or Susan from
The Chronicles of Narnia) set me conspicuously apart. From
grade three onwards, my repeated announcements that I
was a girl born in a boy's body sent shockwaves through
the school. It set the stage for the joking and taunting that
followed. This treatment darkened and intensified when I
told my classmates that I had a crush on a boy named Matt,
who was three grades above me. Matt was a beautifully
handsome and rugged boy, and I was drawn to his athleti-
cism. He was the school jock, but he seemed sensitive, and
his face was really pretty.

I couldn't figure it out at the time. I could only feel the
sharp loneliness that followed me every day. I could sense
that my presence was unwanted, and that even the teachers
and administration had singled me out as different. I was
the odd friend, the weird classmate, the "difficult" child at
home, and the "gifted" student at school. I felt alone even
among most of my friends.

Curiously, the school closed in 2009, a theme that seems to haunt many of the places I studied as a kid and teenager—they literally don't exist any more. It's strangely symbolic since I struggled to authentically exist in those spaces that now don't exist themselves. Visiting these schools that no longer exist is a resounding reminder of the impermanence of suffering. It's all going to be the distant past one day, one way or another.

When I was five and we lived in Chapleau, in Northern Ontario, we were very close to the Fox Lake Reserve of the Chapleau Cree First Nation, and when we lived in Napanee, my elementary school was in the Ontario countryside near the unceded and ancestral land of the Tyendinaga Mohawk First Nation. I believe that being in close proximity to First Nations reserves when I was growing up helped me form a deep respect for First Nations people, and an awareness of the atrocities committed in the interests of colonization. Part of my discomfort with Napanee, and the lack of cultural diversity in my elementary school, could have emanated from a confusion about why white people, including my family, occupied Indigenous land. I stand in solidarity with the First Nations people of Canada. The privilege afforded to me as a white person is one that I will never take for granted. The land I lived on as a kid, both in Chapleau and Napanee, always felt uneasy to me.

Napanee is a very small town. I don't know why we tend to rationalize ignorance by characterizing a town as "small," but many people in town were indeed small-minded when it came to people like me who appeared to be different. I don't want to paint a bad picture of Napanee;

it's a lovely town, and it still holds a special place in my heart. I've learned in my adult life not to judge people based on where they're from or where they live. It's wrong to generalize that all people who live in rural areas or small towns are ignorant, but rural life can exacerbate fear of the unknown and the foreign. Some of the people who lived in Napanee certainly weren't kind to me.

The school was a short distance from our home. I could see it from my front yard, about a ten-minute walk away. I could never get away from the school's presence in my life. The feelings of isolation, being bullied, treated like a freak travelled home with me. I eventually had to come to terms with how my classmates and teachers would look at me. The unconventional child. They would look at me with doubt and suspicion, as if I would somehow destroy their "quiet and comfortable" lives with my uniqueness.

I don't think much of their suspicion and disgust was intentionally directed at me. People can't help themselves sometimes, and it's easy for one child to stand out from the rest. I was the outsider in my school. People talked about little Josh. They whispered about me, had meetings about me, and tried to figure me out. Trying to figure out little Josh never ended, I guess; it continued on until I finally figured me out, and now I find that people trying to figure me out in my adulthood isn't so discomforting.

I was depressed when I started puberty. The thin moustache growing above my lip, the body hair, and other changes created a heaviness in my mind and my feelings about my body. I was carrying the changes in puberty that were meant for someone else. But I had a moment of clarity when I turned fourteen. My trans truth, hidden and confined, broke through the cracks, and I wanted so much to be me. It was the weekend, and I decided that I would go to school on Monday in an outfit that was entirely silver. I thought that duct tape would do the trick, so I used up every last piece we had in our house, and then I went on a hunt for more in our neighbourhood. I knocked on two dozen doors to ask for duct tape to complete my outfit. I was determined to see it through. I find it ironic now that almost every family in my neighbourhood contributed to my duct-taped silver outfit. They had no idea what they were contributing to! I spray-painted my shoes silver, and, like a spell, I also painted my initials on the back of my bedroom door (which was met with a nonplussed reaction from my parents). That day, I began to gather the chrysalis of resilience that would eventually save me. The duct tape was both a representation of my rebellion and my armour.

I wanted to wear this outfit to school to come out to everyone by declaring my diversity on the surface of my body. I used the word "gay" at the time, but I don't think I was ever gay. I just didn't have the word "queer" at the time (other than it being using as an insult to wound me), so "gay" was the next best thing to say. I had come out as gay to my parents, my grandparents, and brothers a few months prior. My family was generally accepting, though they expressed a deep worry about the hard life that I would have to face. None of my friends knew.

I woke up that morning emboldened by my silvery gender expression. I wasn't nervous. My distance from fear was necessary to avoid being trapped in its grip forever.

This was the first time in my life, since my early days of childhood freedom before the gender conversion therapy, that I'd felt free in my expressive spirit. For the first time in years, I had found the courage to be me. I got on the bus with a brave face. And that moment changed everything for me.

Other people's fear, bitter insecurity, bigotry, and rage almost ruined me. I can still feel the sting of their disgust as I stepped onto that bus and sat there for what seemed like forever as we made our way to school. I can still feel the intense energy of stares pouring over my shoulders. "Faggot." "Freak." "Homo." "Fairy." The words would soon become an everyday part of my life. And there were other words, words that used my surname with personal insults to wound me even deeper, like "Faguson." Yes, this highly unimaginative term became the label for me and members of my family. This offence was perpetrated by some very unhappy kids that likely came from unhappy homes in my neighbourhood. I won't name them, though. I won't do to them what they did to me, and they certainly don't deserve to be lifted up in these pages.

The bullying and harassment didn't stop with verbal assaults. When I stepped off the bus, more than a thousand other teenagers awaited me. Why did I think that I would be safe dressed in such an outfit? I was naive to expect kindness from my friends, classmates, teachers, and community. I was so wrong. I underestimated the hate that swiftly accumulated, that was directed towards me that day and for so many days to follow. I was pushed into lockers, tripped walking down hallways, spat on, and verbally assaulted

on a daily basis, even in front of teachers who were supposed to protect me. Not one teacher ever stepped in to
stop the abuse. The bullying was open and explicit. It wasn't
happening in the shadows. No one came to my defence. I
was alone, and pushed severely to the margins, a place no
human being should ever inhabit. I was treated inhumanely.
The school and faculty need to hold that shame for not
taking action.

With time, the verbal assaults developed into more direct and aggressive behaviour intended to rid the school of
my presence. I found the spitting to be the most dehumanizing form of hatred directed at me. I don't know how anyone can spit on another human being, or anything that
is sentient, for that matter. But people began to viciously
spit on me as I passed them in the hallways, or even as I
sat in class. They would also spit gum into my hair on the
school bus. I would have to stand at the mirror later, my
vision blurred by swelling tears, and cut out the gum along
with parts of my hair, freeing myself of their saliva. But I
wouldn't bow down to the hate, and I continued to attend
school throughout this abuse.

And then the vile words, the comments about my genitals, the pushing and shoving and spitting weren't enough.
Some people were now saying that they wanted to kill me.
I began to receive death threats. My peers, fellow human
beings, thought about ending my existence, and they told
me about this desire numerous times.

In the early 1990s, I was one of very few openly gay
people in Napanee. I developed a reputation because of
my outspoken identity and expression, and it followed me

everywhere. My classmates felt emboldened by the inaction of my teachers and principals. Their inaction provided the warrant to mistreat me. As the death threats became more regular, my parents scheduled a meeting with the school principal. Sadly, I don't remember the names of these people, the teachers and principals. They are just spectres to me now, which is fitting, as they didn't really exist in my life other than as apathetic shadows who ignored the inhumanity of my situation. Their silence only made things worse. I was placed in the care of adults who were supposed to protect me and guide me, and they failed. It's shameful.

During the meeting with my parents, the principal told them that the school had never faced anything like this before, and that the faculty weren't prepared to deal with it. Her suggestion—that my parents find another high school for me to attend—only made things worse. The school effectively made me the problem, when I was the victim. I had no real choice but to leave the school.

I feel bad for my parents. The school and the community left them alone to face this issue. It couldn't have been easy for them to know how to help a child who was being verbally and physically abused and threatened daily. My two younger brothers, Adam and James, also had to face the sting of this abuse in their own ways, because my reputation carried over to them. They were attached to the pain and suffering indirectly, and had to attend a school that had forced out their older sibling. Adam, two years younger than me, protected me and my younger brother James as best he could. Beginning to grow into the hulking warrior physique imagined in the role-playing games we used to play in his adolescence (his favourite character was the Incredible Hulk from Marvel Comics), Adam embodied a protector energy, but the number of bullies in our high school was too much for one person to handle. He is also emotionally sensitive, with a bright imagination. It must have been painful for him. I regret that members of my family had to feel of the effects of bigotry. Adam was visiting my Mom and me in Kingston on the night that I was attacked. The image of him hovering outside the police cruiser, in protector mode, while I sat inside being interviewed by the attending officers still makes me feel safe, despite the fact that I was scared to death that night.

When I left the high school in Napanee, it felt like an expulsion, even though none of this was my fault. I was just being me. What came next was a dark time in my life. I was forced to attend a new high school in a much smaller town located between Napanee and Kingston. My experience there ended up being even worse. But, for the first time, people also started coming to my defence. I wasn't completely alone, as there were other "freaks" there who were also marginalized. But I was still a very visible target, even among the other outcasts.

On the final day of my first semester at the new school, the bullying culminated in a dramatic event with hundreds of people outside on the school grounds. About one third of the people outside that day wanted to protect me; mostly they were young women, some of them punks, goths, or geeks, who bravely stood up for me. The rest of the crowd was made up of people who bullied me and wanted me to leave the school, even if it meant taking violent action.

These two groups faced off against each other. Screaming and yelling ensued, and then the bullies started to throw things at us. Administrators from the school intervened, and my parents were once again called into the principal's office to discuss my future.

And they heard it all again. The administration there couldn't handle the problem that I presented. Of course, they weren't officially expelling me, but they told my parents that schools in Kingston, a larger city, would be better able to protect me from the bullies. So, another move to a new school, my third in the span of a year. I felt completely rejected and lost. My depression worsened. I started to fear for my life, but I also started to experience suicidal ideation that increased with the intensity of being dehumanized. The truth of my gender identity and expression suffered because of this abuse. I started to shelter myself, my truth slipped away from everyone: my parents, my brothers, my friends, and myself. I just couldn't be me. I wouldn't allow myself to be me any more. I had to be something else to exist and to survive, and it made me psychologically, spiritually, and physically sick.

I went back into the closet, not figuratively but literally. The closet in my bedroom became one of the only safe spaces where I could escape from the suffering. I would turn off the lights, crawl into my closet, and just shut myself down. I was so hurt, so deeply damaged, that I barely found the strength of spirit to cry. But eventually tears stung my eyes and flowed down my face as I sat in the dark. I wouldn't bother to move anything, and I could often feel the sharp edges of toys beneath me digging into my skin. This space comforted me by relieving the powerful, overwhelming pain I was experiencing. The darkness inside the closet swallowed me up whole. I couldn't see myself, my hands, or my body. The closet became a prison for the screams that I could hear internally shouted out in confusion about the way people were treating me. I would sit for hours in that closet, moving into the corner where I could feel the walls around me. There was nothing and everything in that space all at once. It was my emotional home in pitch-black, where I couldn't see, but I could feel in waves of suffering that overcame me.

Around this time, age sixteen or so, I also began turning to drugs and alcohol to relieve the pain and numb my existence. It's devastating to experience daily verbal and physical abuse. It digs into your soul and drowns your spirit. I was suffering. Throughout my high school years I wanted desperately to just be myself, but other people wouldn't let me. So I stole my parents' pills, took all of the drugs I could find in the schoolyard, and drank to excess. This left me vulnerable in often dangerous situations, and opened me up to another form of abuse—sexual. I'm not saying that substance use automatically creates spaces for sexual assault. But, in my case, it did, and more than once.

THE ONLY WAY TO FIND romantic or sexual connections when I was a teenager was through the first gay chat rooms, simple black-and-white interfaces with the odd picture here and there of a user. I embarked on dangerous encounters initiated in these chat rooms at ages fifteen and sixteen.

I would always lie about my age by a few years, and I had no difficulty getting men in their forties and beyond to meet me. I was obviously a teenager, but my age didn't stop them from taking advantage. I was preyed upon multiple times by men in their thirties and forties who jumped at the opportunity to be with me, to sexually control another human being.

One dark night in Belleville, Ontario, when I was sixteen, a man in his late twenties sexually assaulted me while I was unconscious after a night of drinking moonshine. I woke up while he was violating me and hazily told him to stop. I remember seeing through this mist, a fog, that seemed to be fused to my vision. I didn't have the strength to make him stop. I didn't give him permission. I felt the force of him on me, big and strong, leaving me completely powerless in my drunken state. All I could do was watch the light flicker in the background, numb to what he was doing to my body. I knew that he was acting without my consent, and without my involvement. I recall passing out again, and then waking up in the morning alone in this house where a family was living. I don't remember if he was a friend of that family's, or if I had invited him there. The trauma of the event has blacked out the parts of the assault that seem too impossible to bear.

I had no idea what I was doing. I thought drinking would reinforce my rebellious nature and hopefully numb the pain. But instead it created more pain and psychological wounds. I thought that I was making things better by finding distance from my home, from Napanee, and by meeting these men who would take me away, even if just temporarily. I know that what happened wasn't my fault, even though it felt like it at the time. I was sexually assaulted that night. There was nothing that I could have done about it. I will always carry the assault with me.

That morning, I told my parents what had happened. They responded with tears and anger. How could I have been so careless? They took me to our family doctor. I was feeling things in my body and on the surface of my body that seemed unusual. To this day, I still don't understand why my family doctor didn't call the police, why my parents didn't call the police. I told them not to, but they were the adults and in their eyes I was just a child—a child who had been sexually assaulted. I was scared and confused, and felt dirty and guilty. And my family physician also implied that the assault was somehow my fault with his cold and uncaring demeanour. My family doctor examined me and ran a whole host of tests at the pleading of my parents, who were deeply worried about the possible permanent impact on my health. The HIV test was the scariest. At the time, results took weeks to process. I dreaded that call, but, thankfully, the tests all came back negative.

In the aftermath, all memory of the assault was swept under the rug. I told no one beyond my parents and our family doctor. And I know now that it is a critical part of my story. I was the victim of a sexual assault that night. It happened, and then it happened again in another city with another man just a few months later.

· · ·

I WAS ADAMANT ABOUT travelling to Ottawa by train from Napanee. I had been chatting with an older gay couple from the "big city" who lit up my mind with their stories about living life openly and proudly, visiting bars, and being free with their sexuality. They were warm and friendly, and to this day, I still think they were just trying to help me find relief from the small town of Napanee and the bullying that I was experiencing. My parents tried to keep me from going on that trip, but I was sixteen. I don't blame my parents for wondering why the hell two gay men in their fifties would want to pay for a sixteen-year-old to stay with them for a weekend. It must have been terrifying for them not to be able to keep me safe. I was making very poor choices, and there was nothing they could do about it.

The couple greeted me at the train station in Ottawa. I was a bit nervous to meet them for the first time, having only chatted online and spoken on the phone with them at that point, but it was thrilling to get away from the confines of my small town. They had a beautifully decorated home in an affluent area of the city. I was escorted to the guest bedroom they had prepared for me. The scents of spice coming from their kitchen in preparation for our first meal together hung in the air. And then the smell of alcohol followed. They offered me a drink. I continued to drink for the rest of the night, motivated at first by my desire to loosen up and have fun, and then excited by the new feeling of being surrounded by incredibly attractive men while I was paraded around the bar they took me to.

I was wearing a tight T-shirt with the Batman logo. My hair was coiffed, and all eyes were on me. Fresh meat at the local bar, someone new walked in for their gaze. I remember being shopped around, in a way, introduced to some of the attractive men there by my hosts. I gravitated to a very handsome man in his mid to late thirties with short blond hair, tanned skin, and defined muscles. He had a beautiful smile. I was entranced; no one like this existed in Napanee.

Immediately attracted to each other, we made out at the bar. I think someone told me he was a professional hockey player, but who knows, really. It was all too exciting, and my sexuality felt alive. And that's where the memories fade and the feelings emerge. The rest of the night's details are fuzzy, although I know that we made our way back to the couple's home. I remember feet pounding on the pavement, holding his hand, a taxi ride, and then my clothes were off. Something felt wrong, and I reacted by trying to stop. He kept going. But this time, my body saved me from further harm. It wouldn't allow this to happen a second time. I threw up all over him and the bed. His disposition changed immediately. The smell woke him up from whatever dark vision had fuelled him to keep going when I was so obviously falling into unconsciousness. I cowered to the corner of the room, vomited again, cried, and asked for help.

I was embarrassed and I was scared. I was alone in this big city, staying with a couple who were practically strangers, and I was with this man who should have stopped when I asked him to. The couple and this man tried to calm me down. Likely the fear of what I would do, or who I would tell, terrified them. I was freaking out. They sat me down and offered me a joint. The energy shifted very swiftly in that apartment. They assumed a serious and controlled tone, obviously meant to prevent the emotionality of the experience from taking over and potentially ruining their lives.

I didn't tell anyone about that night, not even my parents when I returned home to Napanee. I worried that they would say they had told me so. And in a way they would have been right: what happened validated their fears. Until I wrote this, only Florian knew about the incident. And only recently, as the #MeToo movement has gained momentum, have I felt the strength to share my experience with others. I watched a television show recently in which one of the characters said something about traumatic stories that resonated with me: he said that he hadn't told his story before because, once he did, he would have to let it go. I don't think I will ever be able to let the stories of the attack and my sexual assaults go, but I do hope that I've treated myself a bit more humanely here by sharing what I had kept secret for so long.

FOUR

The Alchemist

EVERYTHING CHANGED WHEN I began attending high school in Kingston. There I embarked on a journey of self-discovery in an intensive dramatic arts–focused program called Theatre Complete. This was a time of healing for me; I felt safe to exist around people in the program. We were all similar because we were unique in our own ways, and some of us were more obvious outcasts, due to our visible differences, than others. Some members of our group harnessed their truth, owned who they were, and expressed themselves in wildly beautiful ways. The teachers of this program, Al and Susie, created a space for people to be free, to be ourselves—an element unfortunately missing from the mandate of many high school educators, or at least the ones I have encountered. My new school was still a dangerous space, with its own set of bullies who would taunt me while my friends and I smoked in front of the school.

In Theatre Complete I met a person named Eve, who

67

would enter a room and set it ablaze with her intense, focused energy. Everyone was captivated by Eve's honest expression. She was connected to a higher frequency. I had never met anyone like her before. Her expressive fashion sense and free spirit were a salve for me. Eve's infectious spirit brought light and joyful vitality into my life. There were others in that program whose loving energy also acted as medicine. Jana, who shared the healing of music and curiosity of thought with me, and the kind and gentle dancer Beth, who rekindled feelings of freedom through dance that I had repressed from childhood.

I toured around Ontario with Theatre Complete. We performed a play that included a monologue that I wrote about my experiences being bullied as an openly gay teenager. I had the opportunity to stand proud and tall in front of thousands of students in schools across the province to tell my story of resilience. I started to feel strength returning to my body and to my spirit while I was in Theatre Complete. I was still lost inside the pain and confusion, but there was an emerging horizon of hope beyond the illusory protective shields that I had built up around myself for years.

I found my way back to myself by returning to the beginning. I became an alchemist by harnessing all the trauma of dehumanization and hate into a power that I could control. After my studies at Theatre Complete finished, I decided to face my fear and go back to Napanee to complete my last year of high school. I was terrified to go back. Strength had returned to my spirit after Theatre Complete, and the abuse I had faced during the three years I bounced between high schools to avoid death threats and to appease institutions

had given me some very thick armour. But was I truly ready
to face the same bullies who had treated me so inhumanely?
How would I confront these demons? At age seventeen, I
was expressing my gender in an explicitly feminine way,
wearing makeup and adorning my body with unique pieces
of what most would consider feminine jewellery. I wasn't
going to change myself. The classmates and friends who
had been a part of my life during elementary school and
in grade nine were now in their senior year. Would they
welcome me, or continue to abandon the friendships we
had developed during our years in elementary school?

During these years, 2001 and 2002, I kept a record of my
thoughts in a journal given to me by my mom. I wrote a list
at the beginning that highlights a return to myself. The list,
entitled "5 Things I Like About Moi!" included "my creativity,
my values, my individuality, my fashion sense, and my loving personality." This journal, in which I wrote nearly every
night to process my thoughts, is one of the only artifacts I
have from my adolescence that begins to make up for the
many memories that are lost to me. Returning to Napanee
was an important moment in my life, and I wrote at length
about the decision to return to a school that still scared me.
I was focused on myself again at the age of eighteen, but in
a way that I had never been before.

I want to take you through the roller coaster of emotions
that I was experiencing in early 2001. This is when I decided
to take action, to transform the suffering from the years
prior, and to channel it into this new stage of my life — the
journey into adulthood. On January 28, I wrote, "From now
on follow the rules Josh. No more fuck-ups. Be strong."

Two days later, "Today I looked at you in the mirror and you were so beautiful. Your eyes were glistening and full of life. It's inside of you. You just need the KEY." I cried when I recently read this journal entry. I loved myself at that age, despite all the anger, disgust, and hatred directed at me by others.

On February 2, I started to become aware of the defences that I would require to properly protect myself upon my return to high school in Napanee. "Some shields protect, but are shields that necessary? To be open is to be strong. But I might leave myself in too vulnerable a situation. Do what you think will benefit *you* in the most positive, balanced and forgiving way. Think positively of the journey ahead. You are a strong spirit."

On February 5, I wrote, "You made it through your first day. Wasn't so tough, now was it? On with life, on with the march. On with the parade. I am so proud of you, Josh. You have been through so much over the past few years. You have made so many positive, responsible, and mature changes that were very important for your growth cycle. Be strong, Josh. I am the Master of my own life!" On February 8, I noted that "it's been 3 days and not one single negative remark yet. The school has matured and I think it is a visualized reflection on how society is evolving."

My optimistic feelings aside, there were many people who didn't want me back at that school, and I'm sure they were surprised to see me. I arrived back in Napanee unexpectedly, and the administration seemed to be on high alert. My final year of high school demanded a collaborative effort. It was still an unsafe place for me, a dangerous place where I was being taunted and bullied. But I gathered my friends. They were, indeed, powerful people, mostly women, popular in the school, who protected me and cared for me. Their friendship enabled me to complete my final year and helped me to handle the daily bullying. My Amazons were Chantel, Amanda, Becky, and Jenna.

My idea of an Amazon is related to the experiences of many women and non-binary people around me, and is based on a concept specifically learned from Greek myth and popularized by the phenomenon of Wonder Woman. An Amazon, for me, can be a woman (both cis and trans) or non-binary person who does what it takes to survive, who knows what it means to come together with others who might be "others," and who is powerful in their expression. The defining factor is an ability to take a stand and to fight for what is just against misogynistic and oppressive measures. Chantel, Amanda, Becky, and Jenna were strong, fierce, and beautiful young women who carved out their own spaces of respect where only the strongest survived unscathed. I made it through those final months by carefully avoiding the bullying when I could, and dealing with it head on when I was presented with no other options. And I survived with the support of these Amazons.

On February 14, I wrote, "Allies. Powerful allies and powerful contacts." I also noted that I was "back to being the true me. No more being false. Just being true." About a week later, my experience at school made me feel thankful. I listed thanks for life, love, understanding, compassion, strength, friends, enemies, family, for all growing, evolving, and metamorphosing.

I was in a very powerful place in the winter of 2000 at the age of eighteen, facing down the hatred that had forced me to change high schools four times, make new friends, and acquaint myself with new teachers, spaces, and classrooms. On March 1, I wrote of closure on old experiences, starting over, and acceptance of the new parts of my life: "March is definitely a positive-direction month. A time for new beginnings — new beginnings in friendship, work, love partners, change, evolution, appearance, and family. All aspects of my life. Everything evolving. Goodbye to being unhappy. Hello to you. Hello Joshua. Beautiful Josh. I love you." A sketch of a heart ends the passage.

I completed my high school education with many wounds — from my elementary school friends who turned away from me when I came out at fourteen, from the administration and the teachers who shamefully stood in silence and escaped responsibility, and from the bullies who feared so much for their own identities that they tormented me to make their own sick salve. Fear is the root of the poisoned tree that grows within us. Left unchecked, the tree grows and eventually the poison can overtake us. I have empathy for the people who verbally and physically assaulted me during my high school years. I can remember most of them, especially those from Napanee who took out their innermost insecurities and fears on me. I have always been an easy target. To revise a Japanese proverb ("The nail that sticks out gets hammered down"), I am the alchemist, the nail that sticks out and will *never* be hammered down. I have never remained in the position of victimhood. The journal entries from these years show that I never gave up on myself. Every trial and injury that I experienced during high school added another layer to my chrysalis, winding me up tight within myself to protect and empower the core of my soul until the time came to emerge.

IN THE THIRTY-FIFTH YEAR of my life, in 2017, two decades after these experiences, I decided finally to face the trauma of my childhood. With Florian at my side, I visited my old home in Napanee, my first high school, and the school I attended in Kingston. I knew the pain would still be there. But I wanted to process it through the lens of my truth. I knew that I needed to return to my feelings, not just my memories. And I knew that this would never be possible without returning to the physical space where the trauma occurred.

We decided to visit the scene of my attack on the night before we were set to return to Napanee. Approaching from Kingston, I saw the familiar Tim Hortons coffee shop that had offered me shelter more than a decade before. As we approached the train tracks, beyond which lay the ditch where my car was stuck that night, the red lights started to blink and the crossing gates came down. A commercial train roared past us. I would have to sit powerless, very near to the place that brought back so many memories of pain and fear. I sat with my feelings, watching the train cars blur before my eyes. The red lights brought with them conflicting signs. They made me wonder if I should have come here in the first place. Was I doing the right thing, making the healthy psychological decision, in returning to this traumatic site?

I didn't have a choice. I came to the realization that sitting with the trauma like this was part of the process, a preparation. For a short while I was being given distance, while being the closest I had come in a long time to facing my fears. It seemed to take an hour for the train to pass, but finally we were let through. We drove slowly past the ditch, but I didn't feel the need to stop or get out. Driving by was enough to excavate the sharp feelings of trauma within me.

The next morning, we travelled to Kingston. To my surprise, when we arrived at the location of the Kingston high school where I was enrolled in Theatre Complete, there was nothing left. They had completely demolished the school. A crew of construction workers and landscapers were redeveloping the land.

I got out of the car and walked across the street to get as close as possible to where the building had once stood. This high school had provided me with a relatively safe space, among other "different" people, to work through the trauma of being bullied. My time there in Theatre Complete had empowered me to return to Napanee, to face my fears, and complete my high school education. Now standing there, looking at a flattened property, the place I knew in my memories was no longer real. The empty space was a sign to surrender to an important realization: the pain I had experienced when I was seventeen and eighteen would always be a part of me but was no longer real in my present. This was an awakening of sorts that reinvigorated my spirit and prepared me for the next part of our journey, to Napanee.

• • •

OUR FIRST STOP THERE was the old high school. The parking lot reminded me of having to walk to the school bus every day to travel home. I hated those buses. I dreaded the walk from the school, where I was being bullied, to this yellow-orange, old, and smelly bus where I was then forced to endure more abuse—being tripped while walking down the aisle, people's bodily fluids and their chewed gum thrown in my hair.

I took a deep breath and glanced over at Florian, who had his camera ready to document my return. I felt scared and a bit sick. I walked along the pathway in front of the school with Florian following close behind. I came up to an empty and familiar bench. When I had attended this school in grade nine, and then again four years later, this specific bench was always occupied; the space around it was alive. But the spaces that I inhabited alone in grade nine, and then with friends and champions when I returned later, were no longer alive during my visit. There was an emptiness there, like the one I had faced in Kingston. No one was occupying this space any more.

I approached the door and, though classes were in session, it was locked. The school had clearly stepped up the protection and security of its students since I had attended. Just as I started to wonder if it would be right for me to go inside, a student suddenly opened the door for me. I viewed the kind gesture as a spiritual welcome back into the space, a sign to venture deeper into my memories and my feelings. I hadn't been planning on going inside, but this was an opportunity to delve deeper. I looked down the hallway and felt relieved to find people sitting there. They appeared to be finding comfort with each other. The feeling was familiar. At least the space inside hadn't changed much. It was still alive. That made me feel good. But why was I still feeling a sense of fear like I had in grade nine and in my final year of high school?

I pressed on and visited the library, close to where I had spent time with the other "outcasts" at the school in my last year. I now had a Ph.D., and I felt a sense of pride stepping into a high school library that held my memories of academic struggle, when I was unable to focus on anything but surviving the bullying and harassment. I took notice of the graduating-class photos decorating the walls. Excited at the prospect of seeing my own face from back then, and the faces of my classmates, I found the graduating class of 2002. Then a voice from behind me shook me out of my reflection.

"Excuse me, what are you doing here?"

I turned around and came face to face with one of the librarians. I felt the sting of nerves and fear. Was I in trouble for visiting my old high school? What were they going to do?

I calmly explained the reason for my visit. "I'm a graduate. I'm just visiting Napanee and decided to see the school again." I didn't blame the librarian. The school probably had a strict policy for visitors, but I didn't want to announce my presence.

"Oh. You were taking pictures," the librarian countered.

"Just for personal reasons," I explained.

Though cautious and uncertain, the librarian left me alone. I'm sure they still kept a close eye on me while I took a few minutes to soak up the memories. The library reminded me of how small all of this had become in my present, and how big I had become since then. Did I still belong in the small town where I'd grown up?

Our next stop was Springside Park in the middle of the town—a metaphorical stop on our way to my old home. The park has a beautiful little waterfall that my brothers and I frequented with my dad. It's a popular spot for locals and tourists venturing through the area. The sun was at a perfect height to bounce light off the water, warming my heart as I looked up to the sky. I took a deep breath and sat down to write this poem, a reflection on where I came from, and who I had become:

I am the stuff of roaring rapids
White wisps of running water here then gone
Roaring with presence
Taking shape, creating
Keeping safe, searching
I am running, moving, fluid
Made from an element that is neither
Something else, possible, open, free
Limitless power, the stillest peace
Within me, in everything

A short drive from the park took us to my old family home. Standing before it, my feelings were undeniable. This was my home, and yet not my home. I felt a growing sense of paranoia mixed with exhilaration as I looked out at the backyard, the field beyond, and the rock on the hill that I used to sit on top of in my own little retreat. The trees we had planted in our yard were massive, almost unrecognizable. To think that I had once played with my Marvel action figures on its branches, and now they were too high to even reach. I had dreamed about this house countless times since we'd left it in 2001, but now my dreams felt less like reality than I had expected. I knelt down to touch the earth—the earth that had once surrounded the walls of my basement bedroom. I took a little rock from the roadside; I wanted a piece of this place to take with me. I put the tiny rock into a bracelet locket. Why did I feel the need to keep something material from that space? I trapped its energy within a cage; the rock was mine to hold in that moment, taken, and then carried away.

A few weeks later, the rock mysteriously fell out of its little metal cage on my bracelet. To me, that signified that the pain I had experienced in Napanee was no longer a reality. The school in Kingston was no longer there. The bench in Napanee was no longer alive. The elementary school just ten minutes from my home was condemned. It was time to heal by shaping my trauma from within. I don't believe we ever let go of trauma; rather, we work to transform it. We harness it to do better as human beings. We become alchemists.

This is what my short trip to these places was telling me, often in clear and unmistaken ways. Letting go, at least for me, is impossible. But letting go is less about the pain and suffering vanishing, and more about all of these feelings changing their shape to suit who I am now. It woke me up. I was there, all along, deep within a shelter built from the ruins of my pain and the hatred that was directed at me.

It might sound strange, but I am thankful for the night I was attacked. I would never wish that terror upon anyone else, nor would I want to experience something similar ever again, but my spirit emerged victorious. I saved myself from a human being with the face of a violent monster. I didn't have the help of others. I was alone, and I escaped.

I think we all have this power if we need it. It's hidden deep, but I had been doing the work of nurturing it for years, unaware of what was to come. My heart still holds the pain, yet it's not a weakness. It took another decade after my attack to come to terms with myself, to reclaim who I am, but I am here now in these words, and with you in these pages, transformed by my trauma into a loving and empathic human being.

FIVE

The Expression

THE PRACTICE OF ASSUMING gender happens daily for most of us. I've tried to minimize the attention I pay to analyzing bodies in front of me to figure out the gender of other people, but it still happens. I find that I need to snap myself out of this ingrained behaviour. It's just something that happens automatically. I think, why the hell am I still doing this to people, especially considering everything that I know about gender? Did I really need to decide if that person that I just met was a woman, a man, or non-binary? Did I really need to say "woman" while explaining my experience with a person to make my story more clear or understandable?

There is absolutely no reasonable explanation for the need to analyze the gender of my neighbour, my co-worker, or the stranger who just passed me on the street. But I do it anyway, so there must be something preventing us from seeing the full spectrum that actually exists instead of just "man" and "woman."

What happens when you can't figure out a person's gender? For some, feelings of deep curiosity, confusion, or frustration arise. We need to know more, so we fix our gaze to find the solution to the "problem" presented by their mixed gender presentation. It's a problem that dictates the harsh way people judge each other. And, let me tell you, I am definitely a visible problem for some people! Yet I am also invisible. Here's the thing that might seem odd at first: I am both visible and invisible.

It's unlikely that you would miss seeing me when I'm walking down the street. If you saw me, you might look. I visibly disrupt the way you might assume people should look, either as a man or a woman. I look like something else, or at least I like to think that I do, and the gaze of others is often overwhelming. I find it funny, though, that people read me as a woman because they don't want to think about me in a way that might challenge their own ideas about sex and gender.

I get a lot of "sir"s and "madam"s interchangeably: someone might refer to me as "madam," then quickly revert to "sir" when I speak, or vice versa. People are literally mixed up by my presence in person because my gender expression does not register with what my voice or my forms of identification lead them to assume my gender is.

My grandfather has a cute reaction when it comes to reading my gender on a visual level. My grandfather always saw me as a boy, and then a man, until, in recent years, physical changes initiated by my hormone replacement therapy, and my appearances in the press, shifted his understanding of my gender. Pop now, for the first time, addresses me with words of affection typically reserved for women, like "darling," "dear," and "sweetheart." He uses them constantly in conversation with me, and also when he's talking to other family members about me. He also uses both he/him/his and she/her/hers pronouns when he speaks about me, but more often he uses she/her/hers, because I think he actually reads me as a woman, or as I am, even if he doesn't have the correct language to refer to my non-binary identity. His use of she/her/hers pronouns makes it clear that he sees me. My dad finds it funny and cute that Pop calls me "darling" or "dear"; he laughs and smiles because it just seems so natural to my ninety-three-year-old grandfather to say this to me. It's a loving kindness he shows to me, to see me as I would like to be seen. Recently, when I was sitting nearby and searching through my purse for something, he asked my dad, "What is that beautiful lady doing over there?" It is such a feeling of relief to know that my ninety-three-year-old grandfather recognizes me in the way that he can. He isn't *trying* to see me; he is seeing me through a lens of love, and I wish more people could see with love instead of fear.

Some people see me as a trans woman or a woman because I express my gender on the feminine side of the spectrum. Using feminine in reference to who I am suggests that my gender expression might be affixed to the binary. The language to understand gender expression beyond feminine, masculine, and androgynous isn't available yet, or I'm not familiar with it. You may have heard "femme" or "masc" as descriptors for trans identity, or gender altogether. I don't consider myself to be a trans-femme or a non-binary femme. I certainly have an unmistakable femininity, but I prefer to think of my gender expression as being non-binary, not altogether feminine, masculine, or androgynous—a mixture of it all.

My long hair, makeup, and lack of facial hair immediately suggest to many people that I'm either a trans woman or a woman, but I'm not always feminine, or dressed in a feminine way. I don't always feel feminine. It might sound funny, but when I sit with my legs spread apart without realizing (a rare occurance, honestly), I panic a bit, and sometimes cross them immediately to avoid unwanted stares that come from presenting a mixture of masculinity and femininity with the way that I look and how I position my body.

But what do these words, *masculine* and *feminine*, even mean? Well, they don't mean the same thing for every single person around the world. Gender is not determined by things like clothing, hair, and makeup, or by the words, *masculine* and *feminine*. Our gender expression can be determined by these things, but not necessarily our gender. However, we still see these gender cues, and they register as signifiers for gender altogether. I can pass (so to speak), if I want to, with my long hair, makeup, and lack of facial hair. That means that some of the time I can be read as a woman, and I can pass in line with the binary, and how our culture codes gender through specific signifiers like makeup versus no makeup, long hair versus short hair, dresses versus pants, and so on. All of it is conventional and based on very simple ideas that divide people into two categories.

I had an illuminating conversation with a laser hair removal technician (while they were zapping the hairs off my legs) about how my expression automatically tells my gender identity. This type of conversation increasingly happens with people who assume when they meet me that I am a trans woman or a woman. The technician expressed curiosity about my non-binary gender identity. It's likely that they (and, I'm using they/them for this technician because as this chapter suggests, assuming their gender is something I don't want to do) were also intrigued by my gender expression, and how our contradicted assumption makes us question if we truly know everything when it comes to gender. They told me that they had assumed I was a woman, a cis woman(!), when they saw me for the first time. Until I started to speak. My voice disrupted their comfortable assumption of my feminine gender. I have a moderately deep to low voice, so hearing me speak is usually the point at which people suddenly switch from "It's a woman" to "Oh, it's actually a man!" The technician declared, triumphantly, "I had no idea you were trans!" as if to suggest that the contradiction of my aesthetic and my voice confirmed my trans identity for them. I found this experience intriguing and also a bit upsetting. They had switched their thinking about my gender based solely on the contrast between my gender presentation and my voice. I was reminded of how we often think in a very simple way about gender that reduces people to their expression before they can introduce their own identity.

I'm quite visible as a six-foot-tall non-binary trans person with the signifiers that I've shared with you. I'm also invisible as a non-binary person. The truth of my identity is invisible to most people in society. Most people label me as they want to see me just based on my expression, without ever wanting to know how I actually identify. It is impossible for many people to actually see me because some people don't even know non-binary gender exists, or consider it to exist. The person that automatically read me as a woman couldn't see me beyond being either a man or a woman. They read me first as a woman and then as a man, even though they came to realize that I was a non-binary trans person when I explained my identity.

The technician and I ended up having a casual and comfortable conversation together, but when I'm in public, the focused gaze on me is not always as safe as that. There is real danger associated with the gaze when people view me as a monster of sorts that scares or disgusts them. I can make people scared or fearful just based on how I look. Being thought of as a monster doesn't necessarily upset me. I find it kind of fun — it's as if my appearance scares the bullshit out of people that we carry around about gender. A lot of it is made-up crap that we're force-fed from a young age. So, I don't mind scaring the shit out of the gender binary with my expression.

Each day, my gender presentation has to be carefully measured depending on who I'm seeing, where I'm going, and how I'm feeling. I wonder how far I can push my presentation and how much I can be myself. I wish that I could be who I am every single day, but it just isn't possible. Isn't that a sad thing? Perhaps I'm not so alone here. In fact, I know that I'm not. Perhaps you can't always be who you are, either. I'm sure that's the case for many people. As I've said, we are all more similar than we are different.

It isn't always safe to be who I am, or to let my truth be reflected on the outside of my body. I am simply over-whelmed at times by the forces of the gender binary and the pervasive transphobia that can quickly transform the joy that I achieve with my aesthetic into something pain-ful and even dangerous. The gaze that cis women, trans women, and non-binary people — all people affected by various forms of misogyny — face in public can present unsafe scenarios ranging from mild to deadly. I likely don't have to tell you that misogyny is real, or that it affords cis men with a powerful privilege. Some cis men can stare without restraint. And cis men, more often than not, exist without being objectified themselves, unless they are queer and present a gender expression outside the norms of mas culinity. The staring of cis men sometimes evolves into unsafe behaviour — gazing breaches the boundary between looking and unwanted verbal and physical advances. Many other people have made the point that I'm going to make here. Our expression as women (trans or cis), non-binary people, or gender-nonconforming people never warrants the unsafe gaze, verbal harassment, and violent physical behaviour that some cis men practise. We don't have a responsibility to reduce the risk when the gaze upon us turns sinister by policing what we wear, how we walk and move, even how we dance.

My awareness of people's interest in me has increased with my transitioning. The staring in an attempt to fig-ure me out has become more pervasive as I achieve the hybrid body that I want as a non-binary person. The gender-testing that I was subjected to as a young child made me hyper-aware of other people dissecting me in a very inhumane way under their gaze. I became aware of other people looking, whether the looking was harmless or harmful. Both of my parents told me many times to "cool down" the way that I expressed myself. In a letter my mom wrote to me in 1998, shortly after I came out to her and my dad, she said, "We're not always happy with how you choose to express yourself."

I will never forget reading those words in the letter when I was sixteen, or hearing them spoken to me by both of my parents on multiple occasions. I wasn't choosing to express myself a certain way. I was expressing myself my way, the way that I was comfortable doing, and the way that made me feel good and authentic. My parents thought that I was drawing unnecessary attention to myself. My mom sent this request from the depths of love she has for me, and you can read that in her words. She wanted me to be safe. It was a form of protection. But then, in the same letter, they also acknowledged that my gender expression was an essential part of my identity and that it's "hard to be you most of the time."

Being fifteen in Napanee and expressing myself truthfully in the matrix of my parents' opinions, the opinions of friends, the bullying, and who I wanted to be all along was painful. It also wasn't easy being told by my parents that I was trying to prove my difference by dressing a certain way or wearing makeup. This attitude is part of the problem when it comes to accepting non-binary people, especially non-binary youth, because it implies that I would be inviting unsafe attention if I dressed a specific way, and that this unsafe attention, and any consequences that might come as a result, would somehow be my fault.

My appearance has changed significantly over the years and both of my parents are increasingly comfortable with how I express myself. They are proud of my authentic expression, and their cautionary words were always about trying to keep me safe, and came from a place of love. There are some people in my family, though, who simply can't accept me because of how I present myself and my identity, and that is a painful wound that I never thought I would have to bear.

Many parents tell their kids to dress differently because dressing the way that makes them feel comfortable might invite unwanted attention. If only I could wear blue jeans, a T-shirt, no makeup, cut my hair short, and walk with a macho swagger like some assigned-male-at-birth people — a ridiculous notion, I suppose, since not all cis men have to dress or express themselves in this way. Some members of my family (thankfully they are in-laws) have asked me why I don't just live a quiet life as a "gay man" with my cis male partner, instead of coming out as a non-binary trans person and inviting so much attention. Goddess, then my life would be so easy! Why can't I just be like that? Why can't I just be an assigned-male-at-birth gay man who lives my life relatively quietly and peacefully?

Fuck that. It isn't who I am. I've never been one to surrender to the notion that I should dress safely to prevent unsafe attention. And I've been through too much pain in my life from the dehumanization to accept someone else's opinion about how I should express myself and my identity.

In fact, telling me I should be someone else is a form of dehumanization that I never expected from people who I thought cared for me.

My parents' mild protests about the way I dressed during my adolescence, especially when I first came out, have stuck with me, though. They weren't trying to hurt me intentionally. I know that now. I had been sexually assaulted, was being bullied constantly at school, and was severely depressed, even suicidal, so why wouldn't they try to figure out how to help me? And I do find myself wondering if they were right, for that time of my life and that time only, even just a little bit. Am I really saying this? Perhaps it's the part of me that remembers how incredibly painful it was to deal with people's responses to my expression. But this thinking isn't healthy; it makes me assume fault, subconsciously, for the potential risks that I'm taking to be who I am in public. We aren't to blame for the actions of others. We should all be free to be who we are if we aren't hurting ourselves or other people. Of course, many trans, non-binary and gender-nonconforming people, especially people of colour, cannot express who they are because the risk for violence is too high.

I used to be scared to dress a certain way. I've faced some seriously unsafe situations in my life, some that you already know about. Yet I don't want to be fearful of being myself. It feels so good to just be me. I think of it as a battle, which is why I feel like I'm a sorceress from some wondrous realm — a magical monstrosity come from another dimension.

There are many places that are too unsafe for me to visit.

Like nightclubs and bars—I used to love to dance, to just move and connect with my body and the collective energy on the dance floor. The next time you are in a club or a bar, look around at the faces of people who are dancing. The pure joy and freedom on these faces of people, otherwise confined by the rigidity of culture and behaviour, and the expression of their bodies is infectious. Most people love Hallowe'en because it gives us a day to let loose, to enjoy the carnivalesque catharsis (releasing feeling and emotion) found in self-expression, and it's so healthy. Dancing gives us a taste of this freedom that has held meaning in my life, to become less controlled with the way we feel inside and outside of our bodies. Dancing tells an energetic story about who we are and how much we know ourselves.

Clothing also tells a story. My clothes reflect my truth in a fluid way that can fluctuate every day. I dress up most days and put thought behind what I wear, because I want to feel it deeply. For too long, during my adolescence and early adulthood, I was suffocated by the fear of being who I was. I wasted too much time worrying what others would think of me. When I attend professional events—like film festivals, wrap parties for TV shows or films, or other industry events—I feel safe most of the time to dress as I am, since artistic communities can be inviting places for people like me. I feel a sense of deep happiness when I can put together delicious outfits that make me feel sexy, seen, and beautiful. I doubt that I'm alone in wanting to feel beautiful, so here's a story about how my invisible visibility often makes me attuned to a gaze that isn't always safe.

My outfit that night was glorious. I wore tight leather

pants, four-inch platform heels, a transparent lace top with a black bra underneath, and a corset. This was the first time that I had worn a bra in public since my breasts had started to grow. I felt confident and awake, as though somehow my fairy godmother (probably one of my goddess-like grandmothers) had made a visit to bless me with wings for the night. It was a magical feeling. I was living Joshua on the outside, feeling completely free to appear as I am, unburdened by those who feel insecure and who take that out on me. I arrived at this film industry party with my husband, who wore a shiny black dress shirt that had red roses painted on the front. We arrived with flair, as though we were making an entrance at a posh event in an Italian fashion house, empowered by the way clothing can make you feel who you are unlike anything else.

The night evolved into dancing with other artists at the party. Actors often see me, my truth, and share their energy generously with me. This is the beauty of working in an industry where people connect with their own truths and the truths of others to tell a story on screen. I've found friendship with some magical people in the industry. It's the purest joy to be around people who know who they are and who don't see humanity in limited terms. The feeling of freedom while dancing was electrifying.

I became sharply aware that people were also looking at me.

While I was dancing, the staring happened in small waves, and then I began to really notice. There were suddenly multiple people, mostly cis men (because I know who they are), looking at me on the dance floor. They were staring intensely, with no awareness or respect for my space. I started to feel hyper-aware and nervous. Single men who were attending this party weren't the only ones staring. Men with wives standing right beside them were staring. It started to overwhelm me. The staring increased as I became absorbed in the dancing. A few men started to make their way closer to me — many people know this feeling — and I was increasingly uncomfortable as they encroached on my personal space. I looked around me, head spinning like an owl's. Was anyone else noticing what these men were doing? I looked at Florian, who was watching at a distance because he doesn't dance (only once at our wedding!), and I couldn't be sure that he was even noticing what was happening.

They started to converge on me. It felt wild and dangerous. What the hell was happening here, and how could this be socially acceptable? I suddenly became the object of desire instead of the monster — or maybe the monster had become the desired. One of these guys actually started to cross the line on a physical level with me. He began to touch my body from behind with his body. I can imagine that people frequently get away with this type of behaviour in clubs and bars. It was obvious that his touching wasn't related to his dancing; it was being purposely directed at me and to my body. I knew what he was doing, and it was really gross and intrusive. I moved away from him and some of the other guys who were getting closer.

I danced with my friends a few feet away from Florian for the rest of the night. Florian later told me that he did notice the guys who were staring and moving closer to me, which helped affirm what I was feeling and experiencing. It was a relief to know that it had actually happened, that I hadn't manifested it out of my own fear, and that this happens all the damn time to cis women, trans women, non-binary people, and gender-nonconforming people. I empathize with others who must deal with this constantly. This experience won't change the way that I express myself through my fashion, but it has made me more aware of the public attention that I face as someone who not only visibly disrupts the binary, but who ignites a curiosity that some people invade my personal space to explore.

My relationship with being a visible and invisible person grows more positive as our society shifts to accept people like me. I want to be seen. But I also want to be treated like a human being, not an object of study, a sexualized trans body target, or the source of someone's deep-rooted fear.

Pieces of you on me
the projections, the dissections
— they wound me,
yet they also open a space
a place for seeing me
Subject to reject the object
I am open
To be an agent of disidentification.
Stare. Look. Illuminate.
Be aware that I am human.

SIX

The Body

THE BODY IS A COMPLEX SUBJECT for some trans people. It can be a place of pride and self-identity, or the subject of curiosity and questioning. It can be a place of suffering and distress when it does not match the way we feel about our gender identity and expression. And often it can be used against us, to render our identities false; transphobic people attempt to reinforce the notion that we must accept and not betray the body we are given at birth.

It's not up to other people. *Our bodies are our own.*

And yet I don't know of one trans person who hasn't been questioned about their body, their genitals, and their sexuality. I accept that people are curious, but this curiosity often turns trans people into objects of study. This objectification can reduce us to commodities, to fetishized objects, or targets for the projection of fear and disgust.

Trans people are often reduced to our genitals, mostly one or two parts of our external morphology, and the medical procedures that some of us need to minimize the effects of gender dysphoria. These medical procedures, known as gender affirming surgery or gender confirmation surgery (previously called gender reassignment surgery), and the ensuing bodily changes—particularly, those arising from hormones, from facial surgeries, and from top and bottom surgeries that modify genitalia and secondary sex characteristics—have become the focus of the conversation around trans identity. Some trans people require affirming surgery to achieve a necessary and healthy, contented relationship between their gender identity and their sexed body. However, not all trans people undergo gender confirmation surgical procedures.

I have been asked many intrusive questions since coming out as non-binary. If these questions were posed to a cis person they would be seen as highly inappropriate, because cis people are granted more privacy when it comes to their bodies. Somehow, the intense focus on the trans body makes it socially acceptable to ask about our genitalia.

Do you still have a penis? Do you have a vagina? Do you want breasts? Do you still have breasts? Are you intersex? How are you trans if you haven't had top or bottom surgery? Do you take hormone replacement therapy? What hormones do you take? Do you know your chromosomes? What is your sex?

These are just some of the questions that I have had to endure. My attempts to be kind and empathetic in those moments test my patience. Nonetheless, I do try to welcome these conversations in order to broaden the narrative about the body in relation to the diversity of trans identity.

Put yourself in my heels for a second. How would you feel if a total stranger asked you about your genitalia? Would you feel any less uncomfortable if the question came from a friend or a family member? The answer would likely be a resounding no. And that's because it is in fact inappropriate for anyone to pose these questions unless the conversation is welcome. The intent to objectify and reduce trans people to examined bodies—an idea that trans people's bodies are open to objectification and study—renders us less than human. We all have the right to our privacy when it comes to our bodies.

Like most people, I was taught from a young age to treat my genitals as "private parts." Yet the bodies of trans people aren't private. They are somehow dragged into the public realm. Many trans people with public profiles—like Chaz Bono, Laverne Cox, Caitlyn Jenner, and Jazz Jennings—have had to endure highly intrusive and embarrassing moments during live interviews when suddenly the topic shifts to a focus on their bodies, as if nothing else about them really matters. There are many examples of brave trans people meeting these intrusive questions head-on to challenge the discourse and the hyper-fixation on trans bodies. When a trans person challenges these types of questions, it highlights the serious issues with turning trans people's bodies into objects for public consumption. We have become, in a way, bodies to consume, study, and objectify. This focus on our bodies creates a barrier to understanding us as human beings.

• • •

THE CONFUSION ABOUT my body, and the bodies of others around me, was ignited in my first year of high school. Gym class, in particular, made me aware of a deep discomfort about how I felt about my own body in relation to my classmates. Of course, part of this class mandated that boys and girls split up into separate changing rooms. Changing out of my clothing in front of others, making my body public, distressed me.

The requirement to shower in the boys' changing room after class further opened up our bodies to one another. I felt uncomfortable, nervous, and anxious—not only to get naked in front of the boys in my class, but because I could sense that some of the boys also felt nervous and uncomfortable. To avoid this discomfort, I would change in the little bathroom stalls away from my classmates. This led to me feeling isolated, so I spoke with the gym teacher about my extreme discomfort. The teacher self-identified as a woman and her gender expression at the time could have been read as masculine. She was receptive to my request to change somewhere else, so I was allowed to use a private room to get changed before class. The room—isolated, away from the changing rooms—doubled as the janitor's storage space, with mops, brooms, and cleaning supplies. I felt like just another object, an abject "boy" at the margins of the two spaces that weren't meant for me. My classmates saw that I was singling myself out and of course I was talked about. I felt like an outcast of my own making before I'd even realized that I was trans. I often skipped gym class to avoid the issue altogether.

· · ·

I HAVE CONVERSATIONS WITH people about my body when and where I feel comfortable, but for the most part this happens with close friends and family, because I need support from the people in my life who love me unconditionally as a human being. It's a complex experience to live in a body when it is the subject of discussion and investigation.

My non-binary body is my never-ending story. It is a text written with the prose of my flesh—the sensual and the superficial. The non-binary history of my body is layered and etched, and it continues to evolve while my physical and spiritual place in the world shifts. This corporeal experience happens like a communication between who I am and the stories that surround me in the media about other trans people. Three years into coming out as non-binary, a quest to achieve comfort with my body became a central part of my life. Should I transition as a trans person? What does this transition look like if I'm neither a trans man nor a trans woman? How do I transition if there is no fixed gender for me to transition to? These questions continue to affect me with a precise awareness of how others interpret me, how others understand me or want to see me, to place me in the artificial categories of one or the other. And these questions relate to how I understand myself, especially compared to the stories of other trans people.

We feel a need to manipulate the unknown, the unfamiliar, into the similar and recognizable, and so we reduce people to their bodies. The unknown drives fear, and the fear of the "other" motivates hatred as compensation for insecurity. So, in essence, my expression is informed by my body, and its unfamiliar hybridity can be threatening to what we think bodies should look like.

So, am I transitioning? When I was in my mid-thirties, I began to intervene, with medical assistance, to minimize my gender dysphoria and to become more comfortable with my sexuality. But my transition is not a linear journey. I am transitioning without an end point or goal in mind. My gender blooms like the never-ending cycle of the seasons. I don't have a death of self and a rebirth, nor do I have a transition story tied to a beginning, middle, and end.

You wouldn't be alone in thinking that I look like a woman because I wear makeup, have long hair, wear heels, skirts, and dresses, but my body will morph, never the same, over the course of my life.

My mom tries her best to understand who I am. She shows me compassion when trying to understand my gender identity. And still, she and many others tend to think of my gender as either male or female. She's said to me, "Joshua, how are you non-binary if you do all of this work to look like a woman?" I forgive my mom for reducing me to a narrow definition of gender expression to try to make sense of my gender identity. People are swept up in the dominance of the gender binary. I explained to my mom that my expression does not determine my identity. Her perspective is limited by gender that looks exclusively either masculine or feminine.

Indeed, what does non-binary look like?

Well, for one, non-binary looks like me, and it looks like anyone else who identifies as non-binary. Non-binary doesn't look like anything specific, actually, and that is the point. It's the key to understanding us: non-binary people do not have to achieve a certain appearance for our identity to be legitimized. Our identity is not just about our body. And we do not need other people to legitimize our identity for us. Non-binary people can look like anything, the same way cis or trans men and women can look like anything, or should be able to look like anything.

What does a man look like, exactly? What does a woman look like? Our concept of the appearance of gender is shifting, and it has never been the same.

You can't really put your finger on it because these two questions are impossible to answer. Or you could say that the answers to these questions might vary so greatly that they make the point about just how gender diverse we actually are. The moment we start to truly think about what a man or woman looks like is the moment when we start to realize how difficult it is to define gender and what it has to look like.

I WANT A HYBRID BODY to match my fluid gender identity. My sex and my body are becoming more mixed—more non-binary. We have attached the various chromosomes to male (XY), female (XX), and intersex (XYY, XXYY, , and so on), and cis people tend to assume, without specific medical testing, that their own chromosomes match up. But for non-binary people, sex is not always or only determined by chromosomes. Hormonal replacement therapy has created a mix of estrogen and testosterone in my system, achieving a hormone balance that presents in my blood work as atypical for male or female. In other words, my sex is no longer clear-cut.

I began hormone replacement therapy (HRT) in my thirties when I was finally able to confront the pain, confusion, and discomfort that I felt with my sexed body and the way that I enacted my sexuality. Some non-binary people take hormones and others do not, but I think that there is a stigma attached to non-binary people and HRT. There are people, even within the trans community, who question why a non-binary person would even need hormone replacement therapy. I've been on anti-androgen medication (spironolactone), typically used to suppress testosterone, since the spring of 2017. I also started taking estradiol (estrogen) in the fall of 2017. The combination of spironolactone and estrogen started to create what felt like magic waves of change within me. I take those little pills every morning like a potion concocted by some non-binary sage, who sees me and wants me to see my true self in my reflection.

I have to be honest: when I was in my early thirties, I didn't think that I would ever be taking estrogen. I wrote confidently about not undergoing HRT as a non-binary person. I saw other trans people taking hormones, and I thought I would never go down that path. I was convinced that my viewpoint would remain the same. But it changed, and this is the point: our bodies are unwritten stories as we live our lives. Our truth comes to us in time, if we let it. The way I have felt about my body has changed, and it can change for any of us. We don't listen to our bodies enough. We need to learn how to listen to the wholeness that comes when we honour the intimate connections between our body, sex, gender, and sexuality. I like to think of this as my wholeness, my spirit.

I feel as though my experience with the relationship between my body, my expression, and my gender identity was always a battle, but I wage war against my body less now. This is a common thread that unites many of us. Most of us, cis or trans, want to change or alter a part of our body. I've never met a human being who accepts their body exactly as it is. We all make alterations with our clothing, makeup, hair styles and colour, cosmetic procedures, body hair, muscle mass, and so much more. A multi-billion-dollar industry has profited from the common experience of body alteration. Our bodies are an expression of who we are, so there is nothing inherently wrong with wanting to become more comfortable in your own skin.

I questioned for years whether or not I wanted breasts. There were days when I felt as though breasts would make me happy. And then there were days when I didn't want to have breasts, when my flat chest felt comfortable. Then, at age thirty-five, I had a physical epiphany that lined up with my non-binary spirit after taking anti-androgen medication for a few months. I started to feel my breasts for the first time. How could I have been satisfied with such numbness and lack of feeling for so long? The awareness of my growing breasts and the sensations that followed made me feel happy and confident. My entire body became more sensitive—a sensitivity that matched who I was on a spiritual and psychological level. My chest felt like an intimate area for the first time in my life, and the experience with my body for over thirty years of my life shifted. My body began to feel more alive.

I went for a mini-vacation with my husband in the summer of 2017 after I had been on anti-androgen medication for a few months. I packed my swimming shorts, and we ventured off to our retreat at a resort in Whistler. I was an avid swimmer in my youth, and I was excited for the pool. We arrived at the resort and we excitedly prepared for a day of swimming and relaxing. I put on my swimming shorts and a robe. We found a place next to the pool and I sat down on the lounge chair. I felt a shift of attention directed at me and I realized that I hadn't wiped off my makeup from the journey. My long black hair was swept up in a ponytail, my legs were freshly shaved, and I had almost zero facial hair following a series of very painful laser hair removal sessions.

This was the first public place I had been in since starting hormone replacement therapy. I was about to expose my body to others around me, and it all hit me at that moment. I started to feel something new about my body as the attention from others around the pool fixated on me. I sat in the lounge chair with feelings of deepening anxiety. Why was I allowing others to control me like this? What was I afraid of? I stood up and removed the robe I was wearing over my swim shorts. The focus on me heightened into a spotlight. Oh, shit. I quickly raised my arms to cover my chest without even thinking. I'm sure people were expecting to see breasts when I disrobed. I felt that there was something wrong about what I had just done by disrobing in public. I had broken a social code, indeed outdated, standing in that spotlight by the pool that day when I flashed the onlookers.

It's such a problematic double standard that people with breasts must cover up and people without breasts can just bare it all. What is the difference between breasts that can

be covered and those that can't, anyway? I know now that
I felt uncomfortable because this was the first time that I
was aware of my breasts in public. I could feel my breasts
intimately, and it felt odd to expose them publicly.

There are, of course, parts of my body that I'm still
deeply uncomfortable with, particularly my facial and
body hair. Laser hair removal on my face worked to a certain extent, but it is not always affordable, comfortable, or
permanent. And did I mention that it is really quite painful? I started laser hair removal in my early thirties when
my grey hair had already started to appear in places on my
body so I have these very annoying white hairs on my face
that can only be permanently removed by electrolysis. I am
really frightened by this method of hair removal. I had a test
done by a practitioner and it felt like actual torture. I can't
seem to convince myself that getting rid of these annoying
white hairs is worth being electrically shocked hundreds of
times on my face. Perhaps I'll end up accepting them as a
reminder of the forest of beard and moustache that I used
to have, and that used to make me feel so uncomfortable.
Of course, it's wonderfully ironic that my genetics predis-
posed me to very thick facial hair compared to Florian's; my
husband, a cis man, has half the beard that I used to have on
my face! My dad and both of my brothers wear their beards
proudly. I'm glad to be rid of mine, or at least most of it.

Body hair is another interesting component of how we
typically understand and identify gender. I don't think body
hair should determine whether a person is feminine or masculine, or even female or male, and some non-binary people
subvert this false equation. We have fooled ourselves into

thinking that body hair is a strong contributing factor for masculine gender expression and a male/man gender identity. For me, my body hair has less to do with my gender expression and more to do with my gender identity. There is a difference. My body hair reminds me of the pain I used to feel as an adolescent, completely disconnected from my truth, lost and tormented by others. It was the unwanted scraps of reductive biology on my body that betrayed my identity. My body hair does not determine my gender expression, but it does affect my comfort with my own body and how my body relates to my non-binary identity. The hair on my body has also made me feel less comfortable with my sexuality.

I'm not sure that I ever want to achieve a perfect balance with my hormones, my sexed body, and my sexuality. This is not a binary-based subjective experience; human beings are more complex than that. Yet I am finding it easier to be self-loving. The hormonal magic running through my veins is now more hybrid, and this helps me be more comfortable with my sexuality, which I identify as queer, and to explore the edges of language relating to desire, attraction, and pleasure. My heart beats with a magnificent hybridity now; stretching out I feel more in-between, a little less trapped on one side of the binary and within my own body. My fluid gender is now matched with a transitioning towards my own story; the blank pages will always exist, ready for my evolution, in a book that will never read *The End*.

· · ·

FLORIAN IDENTIFIED AS BISEXUAL when we started dating
in 2006. It seems fortunate now to think that I fell in love
with a cis man who identified as bisexual instead of identifying as a gay man. He now identifies as pansexual, which
suggests that someone can be attracted to another person
of any gender and sex. That doesn't mean bisexuality can't
also hold this meaning for bisexual people. And it doesn't
mean that Florian felt limited by being bisexual. What it
means is that he feels comfortable identifying as pansexual.
His identity, too, has shifted over time.

When we first started dating in 2006, no one knew that
Florian was bisexual. He wasn't out to his family, friends,
or anyone other than the people he chatted with online.
The early stage of our relationship involved Florian coming out to everyone in his life, and he was very clear about
his bisexual identity. However, Florian's coming out was
partly based on me and my identity at the time as a gay
man. The early stage of our relationship, sexual and otherwise, revolved around us being a same-sex couple. I now
know this wasn't the most accurate identification of our
relationship.

Here is the essence of Florian, if such essence can ever
be captured by words. He has oval-shaped, deep hazel eyes
that shine with the beauty that exists within him. Born
in Engelberg, Switzerland, Florian grew up more than six
thousand feet above sea level in the Swiss Alps. His height
and broad frame make his kind and gentle soul a pleasant
surprise. He is my prince delivered from the stars. Actually.
One night, when I was about twenty-two or twenty-three,
I was looking up at the stars from my window in my dad's

house. The brightness of Sirius was like a spotlight shining down into my dark room. I was crying. I was so lonely at that time in my life. I looked up to Sirius and asked for love to enter my life in the form of a man who would be gentle, kind, and strong. Florian came into my life through a gay.com chat room a little bit later, just a couple of days after his birthday. The chatting grew into phone conversations and then in-person meetings in Toronto (where he was living with his family). It was love at first talk — before sight! Truly, it is a remarkable gift for our partnership to act as a public example of love beyond boundaries. I am proud to love a cis man who loves me for who I am. We got married four years into our relationship. I actually proposed to him before he could do it! He continues to make so much possible in my life with his love for me.

In my early thirties, I knew that I had to confront how my trans identity might impact my relationship with Florian. He was and is the most important person in my life. We have created a life together, and he is the only person whom I consider when I think about my identity.

None of us can be who other people want us to be, and that includes meeting the expectations of others about our own bodies. I find that, too often, trans people must answer to their family members, particularly when they make decisions about HRT, gender confirmation surgery, or other changes to their bodies. Transphobia from our own family members is a deep and heartbreaking betrayal. I made a strict vow, a promise to myself, that I would never allow another human being, even close family members, to control who I am based on their own insecurities, fears, or embarrassment.

That is their problem, not mine. And their rejection of me is their loss because my existence is based on love.

Florian always had an awareness of my fluid gender identity. The transition from being a same-sex couple to a cis and non-binary couple was a process, and it's still a bit of a journey for us as partners. He says that when it comes to love, desire, and attraction, for him, gender doesn't matter. I just know that love is powerful — the most powerful force in the universe — and that it will always find a way to transcend obstacles.

I IDENTIFY WITH THE TERM *queer* for my sexuality. How I understand my sexuality shifts with time, so this term feels right. Queer is to sexuality what non-binary is to gender, so both make sense for me. Why do we make so many binary-based distinctions about gender and sexuality? We reduce love to either platonic or romantic. Romantic love is elevated high above platonic love for cultural worth in our society, but platonic love used to hold more value. I think we need to get a bit messy when we think about sexuality. Let's mix up our thinking about sex towards a grey area of understanding that different forms of intimacy can be valued in the same way we value sexual intercourse. When bodies are hybrid, how can we continue to think of sex in such simple terms? We think about sex as intercourse, but what about all the other ways that we express ourselves sexually and romantically?

As my body has changed, my perspective on practising sex and self intimacy has also shifted. I used to perform my sexuality as a gay man, and now this doesn't make sense for me. I don't feel comfortable practising my sexuality in a static way. My sexuality feels more free, intimate, and focused on the entire body, not just genitalia. I feel erogenous zones on my body that I've never felt before, and I want to approach my sexuality in new and uncharted ways.

What does sexuality mean when one is attracted to non-binary people who have non-binary-sexed bodies? What is a sexuality that desires non-binary genders, that is attracted to bodies that are neither male nor female? I don't have all the answers to these questions, but I believe they raise interesting issues concerning how we think about sexuality. We can be curious about bodies that are not our own. We can desire and be attracted to bodies that may not follow the normative gendered script of woman/female and man/male, and there is nothing unnatural about this. Our ideas of fixed sexuality and identifying with sexuality based on the binary are crumbling under the pressure brought with more force by younger generations who feel more fluid with their sexuality. Bisexual, pansexual, and asexual identities (among a whole host of others) are increasingly common.

But how does the emergence of non-binary gender identities and expressions further the notion of a fluid and non-binary sexuality? How is it possible to identify with a fixed sexual identity if one is attracted to someone like me whose gender is fluid? What sort of sexualities emerge in relation to non-binary trans subjects? Are we attracted to another person based on their sexed body, their gender identity, and/or their gender expression? Or are we attracted to someone based on all three?

I'll tell you what attracts me as a non-binary person (though it's important to point out that sexuality isn't the same for all non-binary people). I've said that my sexuality is queer, but what does that mean? I think that there are certain signs that emanate from people we are attracted to. These signs stem from our identities. Some of the signs can vary, depending upon one's gender identity, gender expression, sex, and the body. And yet to articulate our sexuality we are forced to reduce our complex feelings about attraction, desire, and pleasure to a very limited range of categories.

I'm attracted to the combination of masculinity and sensitivity. But I'm almost embarrassed to say "masculinity" in this context because it seems so simple and reductive when I know that there is an infinite array of gender expressions existing among human beings around the world; limiting it to just "masculinity" seems misleading. It's more comfortable for me to say that I'm attracted to masculinity and to people who identify as men than to say I'm pansexual like Florian. But masculinity means different things to different people, so I want to dig deeper, beyond that term, to discover more about my sexuality.

There is a difference between how I *think about* my sexuality and how I *feel* my sexuality. My thinking about sexuality is constrained by the limitations of language and the inability to articulate gender expressions and genders beyond the binary: masculine, feminine, or androgynous, and then man, woman, or non-binary. The way we think about everything is constructed around this dynamic, and yet I feel my sexuality deeper than what my conscious and rational mind can put into words. The term "non-binary" emerged in response to an erasure of gender beyond the binary, so hopefully new language will eventually arrive to help explain sexuality in richer ways, to match the ways in which we experience our sexual subjectivities.

Heteronormativity is a dominant force that prevents some people from realizing love in an honest way. Sexuality is so much more than what we think it is when we allow it to be defined solely by a binary idea of bodies and the love and attraction that is supposed to match up to those bodies. We enact our sexuality through our bodies, but the body is our own. It shouldn't be used as a barrier to prevent us from loving who we desire, who we are attracted to, and who we care deeply for. I'm proud of what my relationship with Florian represents. He loves me for who I am—not necessarily the body that was expected of me or that I was born into, but my body for what I want it to be. My home.

SEVEN

The Empath

FROM MY EARLIEST MEMORIES, I can remember sensing emotion, pain, and suffering in others. People have often remarked about my hypersensitivity and my empathy as if I exist on an altogether different frequency. I can't avoid seeing and feeling the suffering of certain people. In my adult life, I've found ways to manage the emotions and energy that I soak up, while navigating my own persistent experience with suffering and depression.

Depression and empathy have become synergistic for me. I fight my depression because it doesn't feel good to suffer. I'm self-critical when the depression takes hold; I feel guilty for surrendering to sadness and exhaustion. But I'm learning to accept my depression. It's a part of who I am and who I've been since my pre-teen years.

I would like to think that what we feel is complex and beyond a binary understanding of emotional subjectivity. My feelings are more grey than black or white, in between instead of good or bad, happy or sad. I'm sure that many people connect with the grey area of feelings. If I continue with this line of thinking, then my depression is neither good nor bad; it just is. I can't control my depression, but I can work to alleviate my suffering by minimizing my resistance to it. I suffer greatly in trying to resist depression because by doing so I'm trying to control it. I can't control my depression or my empathy. I have been told many times in my life that I should try not to be depressed, as if I can simply flip a switch through sheer willpower. Accepting my mental illness is not about surrendering to it and letting it ruin my life. Instead, accepting it as a part of who I am allows me to work through my feelings. My depression opens many empathic windows to affect other people in positive ways by extending compassion.

Why do I try to explain or rationalize my depression? Why do I need to understand why I feel depressed? I guess I'm trying to find comfort by understanding the darkness and numbing sadness that can work their way into my life to suffocate my clarity, my happiness, and my outlook. I don't know exactly why I have to deal with depression more days than not, and I don't think it truly matters where my depression comes from in order to accept it as a part of who I am. My depression is part of my existence in this world. To some extent, it has always been with me. It is a part of me, but it isn't all of me, and it doesn't completely define me. For once in my life, I would like to be fine with accepting the fact that depression is part of my life.

I experience gender dysphoria alongside my depression to varying degrees every day, but let me be clear that my gender dysphoria is not a mental illness. Dysphoria relates to both thinking and feeling, the latter being slightly more difficult to explain. There is a disconnect between the feelings I have about my gender, the state of my body, and my ability to feel whole as a human being. The wholeness that is achieved when I feel less dysphoric is spiritual. I feel one with energy and humanity when I feel together, less uneasy about the relationship between my mind and my body. Being fluid is like being out of the social order, but in a healthy, liberating way with room to breathe, since being socially ordered can feel suffocating. Tapping into a fluid gendered subjectivity gives me space to connect with my body, mind, and self because everything is in constant change. Dysphoria is a part of my process; it makes me aware of the subtle shifts, and it prompts me to be fluid and open beyond the cultural constructs that aim to reduce me to a simplified entity.

I can't always decipher emotions that I'm feeling, or the feelings of others that I've absorbed without really being aware that it's happened. I can sense thin layers of energy that separate me from other people. We are all made up of a variety of energetic forces that come from the same source. Beyond the energy and emotion existing in every human being, my experience with empathy, and later spirituality, was shaped by the suffering of those around me, especially the people closest to me.

Recently, my mom said, "Joshua, I treated you like glass when you were a baby." I spent a lot of time thinking about those words, trying to understand their meaning. Had she been afraid to break me because of her own childhood and adolescent trauma? Had I really been that delicate, or sensitive, to be broken so easily? I was her first child. My parents treated me carefully. Yet I can't help but think that this metaphor signifies an empathy that I demonstrated from a young age; she might have understood that even as a small child I could sense her feelings.

My mom balanced the world around her in a way that hid the enormity of what she was actually doing for our family. I still find it difficult to explain how she managed to care for us while working full-time as a psychiatric nurse. She was always working, it seemed. Her job at the hospital required her to work a chaotic shift rotation of early mornings, afternoons, and nights, and still she managed to keep the house clean and tidy, drive me and my siblings to all of our various extracurricular activities, manage a small business with my dad, extend emotional support to me, and even volunteer at our elementary school. My dad certainly helped with everything. But my mom seemed to carry a weight and responsibility that, though it was always obvious to me, I never fully appreciated until I became an adult.

Her depressive episodes weren't as apparent to me while I was growing up. She hid that side of herself from us. It must have taken an enormous toll to wear that mask whenever her depression got bad. My mom went above and beyond. She is the exemplar of motherhood in my eyes. She saved my life, many times. I'm not so sure that I would have been able to survive everything—all of the bullying and suffering—without a mother who loved me as much as she did, and continues to do. She sacrificed part of her own happiness and mental well-being for me and my brothers. I know it.

When I was in my late teens, nearing the end of high school, I started to sense a disconnect in my parents' relationship. Something sad and ominous had emerged. My mom began going out late at night after working an eight- or even twelve-hour shift and coming home at one or two in the morning. Sitting in our cold garage like a gargoyle, cemented in place by my concern, I would wait for her to get home. I needed to be there for my mom in those moments, to make sure she got home safely from whatever it was she was doing out so late. I knew what was happening, but I didn't want to admit it. I wanted her to tell me and to tell our family. I had watched enough drama on film and TV at that point to know what can happen to a marriage.

One night, when I was eighteen years old, she came home at about one in the morning and found me sitting on the stairs in our garage, chain-smoking. It was a cold winter night. She drove her car into the garage, and I could sense that she was scared to see me. I could see the sadness in her eyes. Perhaps she was afraid to reveal to her teenage child what was really happening during those late-night adventures. What parent wants to talk with their child about an affair?

I was feeling her absence for the first time in my life, and at eighteen I thought I had a right to know why she was suddenly disappearing. I wanted to know what was going on. I knew she wasn't happy, but *why* wasn't she happy? Did she no longer want to be our mother? What propelled her to take such risks, driving home late at night with booze on her breath? And why was she suddenly not there for my younger brothers, who needed her as much, possibly even more, than me? I didn't want my family to fall apart. So much of my life had already been difficult enough, and I was depending on the stability of our family.

She walked up the stairs towards me. Part of my mom was absent in that moment; she had disconnected to protect herself, and possibly to protect me from the truth. I looked down at her, visibly shaken, and asked her to tell me what was going on.

"Are you cheating on Dad? I'll understand if you aren't happy, but you can't lie to me. Please tell me the truth. I won't forgive you if you lie to me."

Her answer to my question haunted me, and our relationship, for years. She brushed past me and said that, no, she wasn't having an affair. It was an obvious lie; her eyes told the real story. I felt betrayed.

Finishing my cigarette, I sat there alone for a moment, cold and confused. She had lied to keep me safe the only way she knew how. What was happening in her life was too mature and complex to share with me, and it was also private.

I followed her into the house and my dad came out of their bedroom. He must have been waiting for her to come home as well. I stood in the kitchen feeling trapped inside a triangle of emotions, with my parents standing, apart from one another, in our home where we had spent over a decade eating, laughing, and sharing our lives. The space suddenly turned dark. Those memories were now in the past, and this was my present, with my two younger brothers sleeping soundly, unaware of what faced us, downstairs. I couldn't escape the reality of my parents' fracturing relationship, and how the cracks in their foundation would affect me, Adam, and James. There weren't many words used that night. Nothing was revealed, yet I had a feeling that everything had been said.

The year that followed was a living nightmare, as our family's story entered an even darker phase. The end of their marriage was marked by a story of betrayal that seems almost fictional. It was a tale written with my dad's depression and his broken heart, and the extreme guilt that my mom felt for leaving him, and our family, for someone else. When the truth finally came out, my dad was utterly devastated. I understood the betrayal he felt because my mom had kept the affair hidden from him.

During a sunny fall day, the skies went dark on our family. Our tiny neighbourhood in Napanee was transformed into what must have looked like a movie set to people driving by. Dozens of police officers surrounded our countryside home and cordoned off our street. Their mission: to save my dad's life.

My dad had locked himself in his bedroom. In fact, the door had been locked the night before, and as I'd made my way to bed I'd heard his loud cries as he talked on the phone with a counsellor. He'd spent months on end shut in that room. At first, if I asked, he would let me in to be there for him, to support him. But in those final few days before the suicide attempt he had completely isolated himself.

I knew there were guns in the house for my parents' hunting adventures for moose, deer, and duck. When I knocked on the door that dark morning, he yelled out that he was going to take his own life with a shotgun. You can never free yourself from the feelings that are created when a parent tells you they are going to end their life. It sticks with you, it shapes you, and opens you up to feeling what someone you love is feeling.

The pain and the sudden grief were sharp and might easily have frozen me in place. But the survivor in me immediately thought of my brothers. They were young and they were afraid. I needed to be there for them. I needed to control this situation. I called 911. The response was fast. I gathered James and Adam and we spent almost an hour, what really seemed like forever, waiting across the street at our neighbours' house, standing in their yard, me chain-smoking, all of us staring across the road at our home and the dozens of police officers gathered there.

I felt an instinctive urge to think about the situation more deeply, to analyze this nightmare in front of me. How could we lose our father like this? We couldn't. What was really going on? Then I realized that the shotgun might have been an excuse to get me and my brothers out of the house. My empathic connection with him, already strong from weeks of being close to his suffering in our home, made me realize that he had likely taken pills that were kept in the en suite bathroom.

I ran down the neighbours' long driveway to a police officer conveniently parked at the end, likely posted there to keep me and my brothers away from anything that might have happened at our home that day. Out of breath, I explained that my dad had taken a bottle of pills and they

would need to get him medical help before he overdosed.
The police reacted quickly. They told me they were listening in on the phone, and my dad had been trying to call my
mom at work. His voice had sounded drugged.

I made my way back up the driveway to be with my
brothers and our neighbours, and then we received a call.
He was telling us on the phone why he couldn't continue.
He took turns saying goodbye to each of us. That goodbye
will stay with me forever. I never thought I would hear his
goodbye until I was old. This was happening too fast. He
couldn't leave us behind.

I knew the officers were listening in on the call, so I told
him directly that I knew he wasn't going to use the gun, if
there was even one there, and that he had taken pills. He
admitted it, and minutes later we saw the officers carrying
him out our front door on a stretcher and putting him into
an ambulance. It all came down to that moment. Was he
still alive?

He told us later that the phone call with us had woken
him up. He'd decided he wasn't going to die like that. With
what little strength he had left, he would try to save himself. He told the officers that he would open the door, and
when he did they pushed him to the ground, unsure if he
had a gun or not, and called in the paramedics to give him
emergency medical attention. The ambulance rushed him
to the hospital. Me, my brothers, the officers, the paramedics, doctors, even my dad: we all played a part in saving his
life that day.

I sat on a bed that evening in the home of one of my
father's friends. With the door closed and an address book

in front of me, I called dozens of people, family members and my parents' friends, explaining what had happened and reaching out for support. I spent hours on the phone talking about the incident over and over again until it became a script that I was reading. I became emotionally detached—I had to in order to remain composed and deal with a responsibility beyond what would typically be expected of an eighteen-year-old.

I still feel that day as if it happened yesterday. I don't blame my dad. I forgive him. I understand why he called out for help. And his suicide attempt brought me closer to him and his feelings. It strengthened my bond with him, which hasn't always been solid, and it made me feel a depth of suffering that enriched me as a human being, helping me to see and be there for people I love as the empath that I've come to be.

That wasn't the end of the nightmare that month for me and my brothers. Three weeks later, at the end of her emotional rope, my mom sat in her car looking down at the contents of a bottle of clonazepam tablets sprayed out across her hand. She was considering taking her own life. She was suffering from severe depression from an undiagnosed bipolar disorder and the guilt she was feeling about my dad's suicide attempt, and now she was experiencing suicidal ideation herself. She, thankfully, had a last-minute change of heart, thinking of me and my brothers. She called to admit herself to a psychiatric ward. I only recently learned this part of the story when I opened up the memory to write this out.

That month, my brothers and I had to visit both of our

parents in the hospital. My mom ended up in psychiatric care, which was where health care professionals finally, thankfully, discovered that she had bipolar disorder. In their absence, I assumed the position of caretaker for my brothers for months while trying to finish my final year of high school.

Visiting my mother in the hospital gave me the opportunity to see her vulnerability. She was normally so strong, so composed and controlled. She had wrapped herself up to contain the trauma of her own life in order to take care of us. Her weakened state was paired with a power. After all, she had saved herself in a very lonely place, guilt-ridden and ashamed. She never wanted to hurt us. She never wanted to hurt my dad. I was proud of her for surviving her suicidal thoughts, burdened by the instability of her illness.

You never entirely move on from your father telling you goodbye on the phone and talking about a shotgun while you are forced to watch from one hundred feet away, at the neighbours' house, after he has swallowed a bottle of pills. And you don't ever get over seeing your mother suffering from her mental illness in the wing of a psychiatric ward. She was always so strong, and she fell apart into unrecognizable pieces.

I was eighteen years old when we almost lost both of our parents in the same month. Ours had been a picture-book, small-town family — albeit one with a queer child — but then everything changed. The story, our story, swiftly spread through the rumour mill of the town. We had been known for notable academic, athletic, and creative accomplishments. My parents were successful people with professional careers and a small, profitable business on the side. They hosted many lovely dinner parties with their many friends and made vital contributions to the school and the community. Then everything fell apart—their marriage, our home, and my relationship with both of them.

Today, my dad feels a potent mixture of shame, guilt, and embarrassment. He has a difficult time talking about that time of his life, and how it affected me and my brothers. The end of my parents' relationship, the way that it played out, took a significant emotional toll on him. It would have exacted a significant toll on anyone. Within a short period of time, he lost everything that he had built over decades with our family. He witnessed his whole life crumbling before his eyes. The weight that men carry in our culture can sometimes be suffocating and overwhelming. There is a pressure to uphold expectations, to hide the vulnerability and emotion that all human beings should be able to experience without guilt. His shame is a spectre that is a difficult and traumatic part of his history and our family's history to this day. But I'm also proud of the way he has transformed from the darkest day in his life.

After my dad's suicide attempt, his counsellor told him something that bears remarkable similarity to my own experience of reclaiming myself through the power of spirit and empathy. The counsellor told him to find "little Mark" again, just as I have had to reclaim "little Joshua" to be who I am. My dad was lost to himself from the decades spent in what he sees as a codependent relationship. It is a powerful practice to reconnect with who we were prior to a lifetime of repeated trauma and increasing dependency.

One of the challenges for me was confronting some of my extended family members, who felt powerless to help my parents through this dark time. It was a darkness that felt too real for them. I had experienced my fair share of gloom, but I hadn't distanced myself from it yet. I was still situated deep within my own trauma. I hadn't found the balance of compartmentalization that in adulthood often helps us to develop coping mechanisms. I was there for my dad in a very conscious, clear, and active way. Yet my relationship with my mom suffered for years because I chose to focus on my relationships with him and with my brothers. When families separate, it's difficult for kids to stay close with both parents. Children are often forced, impossibly, to choose a side.

My mom had the strength to live and function through manic depressive episodes for most of my childhood. She is another Amazon in my eyes, a survivor, and an inspiration. I don't ever want her to feel guilt for breaking free from the confines of her marriage. I can't judge what was done in their relationship, nor do I have a right to. I don't need to know the intricate workings and failings of their relationship. I thought that I had a right to know about the truth of her affair, but I now know that I didn't have that right, and that she was also trying to protect me.

My mom and dad will always be my parents, even if they aren't together. My mom needed to make a change in her life. She needed to move on from a life that she no longer wanted. I wish that I could have simply said to her that night in our garage, "I'm here. I love you, and I will always respect you, no matter what." But I've said it to her now, many times, and she knows it.

My parents weren't perfect. I don't believe any parent can meet all of our expectations. They show us their humanity in their mistakes. And I learned the most from them when they became human beings to me, not godlike figures on a pedestal. These events shaped me, made me more brave, courageous, and self-sacrificing. And what happened to us opened a door to a more powerful empathy, because I could see my parents as the human beings they are, not just as who they wanted me to see. Their mistakes helped me forgive the mistakes of others, and to forgive myself in the moments when I almost slipped into dangerous suicidal feelings. Most of all, their survival strengthened my spirituality, made me aware that there are powers beyond, infusing us, protecting us, and at times perhaps testing us.

MY PATERNAL GRANDMOTHER, Nan Thelma, also expanded my ability as an empath with her own depth of intuition and sense of spirituality. She was the most spiritual person in my life, a deeply faithful Christian who worshipped in the Anglican Church. Sadly, she suffered severe physical and emotional abuse as a child, and I could always sense this suffering in her. Nan Thelma was one of my best friends. She was a dear confidant and companion. She was a survivor who faced many challenges throughout her life.

As a child I sent her handwritten letters, and in my twenties and thirties I spent hours with her on the phone. Her warm voice came from the love she kept for me in her heart, and it always made me feel special. There wasn't a moment in my life when I didn't know how much she truly cared for me. At the end of my phone calls with her, she would always tell me that I would be in her nightly prayers. She would remind me that her angels would always look after me. Her spirit passed on when she was ninety-one years old. She is one of those angels now, perhaps the most powerful one, a guiding and protective energy lifted up by the love she shared with me throughout her life.

I adored my grandmother for her elegance, beauty, and quiet strength. Her Dietrich-esque eyebrows pencilled with precision, her body adorned with furs, chic shoes, and gold accessories. Her presence emboldened by a scent of sophistication thanks to Chanel N° 5, and her sharp, manicured nails accentuated further by extra-slim menthol cigarettes. She was a powerful role model to me of femininity and grace. I always wanted to be physically close to her during visits, as if her feminine elegance, strength, and intuition would somehow rub off on me.

When we knew the end was near for my grandmother, I didn't want to say goodbye to her, but I had to see her in person before she passed to express the depth of my gratitude for her love. And I'm glad that I did, because my last moments with her ended up being the most beautiful and meaningful of our life together — a life full of laughter, smiles, and conversation. My last moment with her was a spiritual experience that highlighted the power of faith, not just in ourselves but in the people around us, and cemented our empathic bond forever. I can't put it any other way than this: Nan Thelma said hello to me on the day that we also said goodbye to each other in this life.

"Goodbye, Nan. I will miss you. Thank you for loving

me and for always being there for me," I said to her with hesitation and sadness at the end of my visit in palliative care.

I sensed a sudden wave of energy as she looked into my eyes and said, "Be a good girl, Joshua. Be a good girl."

Oh, my goddess, I can't believe she just said that, I thought as soon as the words left her mouth. I froze in that moment and looked at her with a widening smile. Here she was at ninety-one years old, recognizing me as a trans person in the best way she could. Seeing me with empathy, making me feel respected and appreciated. My grandmother gave me the greatest gift when she greeted me — the real me — for the first time, and on the level of language.

Being seen as I am by people is a remarkable feeling, and my grandmother gave this gift to me in the most unexpected moment. I wanted so much to tell her that I appreciated her for seeing me. How did she know to say this during our last conversation? Nan Thelma always knew when I was trying to hide difficulties in my life. She could always sense my suffering with depression and the uncontrollable effects of being an empath. She was inquisitive and curious. Sometimes, she would gently nudge me on the phone and encourage me to explain what was bothering me, even while she was experiencing her own physical and emotional challenges. Her last words to me made me realize that our goodbye wouldn't last forever. "If things get tough," she said, "I'm two steps behind you, always there."

We don't ever lose the ones we love. They join us on our journeys through life. The memories they imprinted upon us, the love they shared with us, and the appreciation and respect they had for us continue in a way that we can always count on. My Nan Thelma will live with me for the rest of my life—just two steps behind me—while she embarks on a new beginning of her own.

I found her Bible after her passing. Tucked into the front pages, among some old news clippings, was my birth announcement. When I read it, I was struck by the discovery that there was no mention of my sex or gender—something that is almost always included in such announcements. I took it as another sign from Nan Thelma telling me to be who I am. It was a sign from beyond, knowingly felt thanks to the empathic cord always connecting us.

My maternal grandmother, Nan Lois, was also a formative force in my life, and we also shared a deep empathic connection. Like my Nan Thelma, Nan Lois was a star; when she walked into the room, everyone turned to look at her. She had platinum, almost white blond hair, a statuesque body, sharp nails often decorated with crystals in the polish, and a golden tan. She had an effortless flair for style, and she looked glamorous even in plain white T-shirts that she would sometimes wear without a bra. This look stuck with me as a kind of empowered beauty since it seemed she was unafraid to show her body. I'm inspired by her expressive power, and the power she felt in her body. I often think about how powerful I would feel if I had a similar body.

Her death at seventy-three, after a long battle with breast cancer, left me with a grief unlike anything I had ever felt. We had spoken a few nights before she passed. She was in York, Pennsylvania, and I was in Ottawa at the time. I was planning to visit her in the hospital, but she died unexpectedly the day before I was to arrive. I had heard in her voice a few days before that she was very ill, and I could hardly bear the sound of my strong, direct grandmother in this weakened and confused state. I can still hear her and the force she gathered to tell me one last time how much I meant to her and that she loved me. That moment lasts forever.

I discovered in my mid-thirties, from a news article published in 2011, that she was partly responsible for ending the reign of a notorious sexual abuser in Pennsylvania. Allegedly, this lawyer had assaulted my Nan Lois one day in a bar. He messed with the wrong woman that day. Though he had never been charged, there was good reason to believe that this lawyer had sexually assaulted both clients and members of the public. My brave grandmother hired her own lawyer and sued the man for sexual assault. This was during the 1990s when sexual assaults were rarely reported, a far cry from the current focus and attention generated by the #MeToo movement. This man was eventually disbarred for his actions. The news article stated that his disbarment, and the ongoing litigation to secure damages for victims, was partly a result of my Nan Lois taking legal action and speaking out against the assault.

I had never been as proud of my grandmother as when I discovered her bravery. I wish that I could've told her how much this meant to me, for her to take action and to speak out against sexual assault at a time when there was so much silence around it.

My Nan Lois also taught me how much I could learn from self-love, a likely consequence of being the victim of abuse. I have an undated letter, sent at some time in my childhood, that came with a notepad. She wrote, "This is to keep a daily journal. If you do this you will be surprised how much you learn over the years. Love you, Nan." Well, I like to think that this advice informed even these pages.

I'm the descendant of a long-line of Amazon women: my grandmothers, my mom, and looking further back there were other strong and powerful women in my ancestry. My grandmothers both suffered deeply, and somehow I knew this from a young age. My empathy has been inspired by the powerful emotional connections shared with both of them. Some cultures believe that trauma is intergenerational, that the suffering travels through the bloodline, spirits, and energy across generations. I am a mosaic of suffering, then, but also of resilience.

I WAS BAPTIZED in an Anglican church when I was a baby. I don't feel connected to the Christian faith specifically, but I do sense an undeniable energy when I walk into churches, particularly those that have existed for centuries. I feel magic in older churches. They are filled with an emotional energy: sadness, hope, joy—an endless array of feelings left behind. The concentrated energetic faith also pulls me empathically to these spaces. Like the prayers that are spoken in churches, each energetic force gets trapped, like little stories mapped in the varied architecture of emotion and energy.

My secular spiritual faith, combining parts of Christianity and Buddhism and involving a practice of compassion, respect for sentient life, and the power of prayer, is related to my empathy. The power of my spirituality, a force of empathy really, comes from a source beyond that which can be fully contained in language. Practising spirituality, and my connection to energy, involves a deep desire to know that there is something more than our daily lives, something that we can believe in and channel our faith into by releasing ourselves from the incessant and repeated suffering of life. The need to always categorize our spiritual existence prevents us from finding a similarity in our faith. At my core, I have learned from experiencing my suffering and the suffering of others closest to me — like my dad, mom, and grandmothers — that faith and hope can be life-saving, and they can inspire us towards tolerance and love for one another.

Florian grew up in a small village in Switzerland called Engelberg, which translates as "angel mountain." It's the perfect name to describe the special, almost magical feeling one enjoys when visiting there and spending time with the village's beautiful people, who live with faith in their hands and hearts. The origin of Engelberg dates to the year 1122, and it's the site of Florian's ancestral heritage. The village sits at over three thousand feet above sea level almost in the middle of the Swiss Alps. Another three thousand feet above this village, near Lake Trübsee, is where Florian grew up. We named our production company Turbid Lake Pictures after the English translation of Trübsee. Florian had to travel on a cable car every day back and forth to his school in Engelberg. You can stand anywhere in the village and look up at a panorama that perfectly resembles a majestic painting. It's truly that beautiful.

Visiting Engelberg is a spiritual experience. Aside from its natural beauty, the village has a spiritual force that resonates from its Catholic monastery. I cry every time I visit the massive church with its marble altars. I can feel on the edge of my skin the waves of energy that have been left by the spirits who once resided there.

The first card I gave Florian, a month after we started speaking on the phone, had a picture of a lighthouse illuminating a hopeful horizon. Florian became that light in my life. I wrote to him in that card in April 2006, "Even though we haven't met, I feel like we have in a way. The light on the front of this card reminds me of you." In a letter to me from him in 2012, he wrote about us being "unstoppable together."

Florian is a special kind of soul, and I understood this even more profoundly when I met his grandmother in Engelberg, Helen Hess. She was the picture of kindness and respect towards me. I first met her in 2009 when Florian had only told his parents and brother about his relationship with me. The rest of his family in Switzerland didn't know at that time. His Mutti (the Swiss word for mother used affectionately by Florian's family for his grandmother) embodied a strength and resilience that reminded me of my own grandmothers. She gave me three kisses at the end of our first visit. She then looked up at me with a gratitude that I felt deeply. A connection was formed as we looked into each other's eyes. I think she saw my love for her special grandson. She could feel it through me. She then said to me, "I know. It's okay." I took that as an acceptance of our relationship, even though Florian hadn't told her about us.

He was understandably nervous about telling his family there, considering the family's traditional Catholicism. I told him right away what she said to me and he seemed deeply relieved. While speaking to her on the phone just days after we returned from our first trip, he came out to her about our relationship and his sexuality. I remember vividly that she told him life is all about love, and that's all that matters. She could see our love.

We proudly wear the wedding rings she bought for our marriage a couple of years after that visit. We then travelled back to Engelberg again to explore opportunities to shoot a film in Switzerland, but during that trip we made special memories with her, unafraid to be honest about the love Florian and I shared with one another since she had shown us such unqualified support and love. She enjoyed having conversations with me in English. Our few days in the village were spent walking with her and her sweet dog, Wanda, and going out for lunches that she eagerly awaited.

We ended up travelling back to Engelberg, our third visit to the village together, to honour her life when she passed away in the spring of 2018. I'm fortunate that Florian's uncle, his cousins, and family friends have also accepted me. They welcomed me with open arms at Helen's funeral. It meant the world to Florian, and it warmed my heart to know he could mourn the loss of his grandmother while still feeling loved.

I don't know for certain if Helen completely understood my identity—we came from such different generations and cultures—and I don't think it really matters in the end, because she simply valued and accepted me. I think Helen elevated this love and respect partly because of her spirituality, and how her spirituality informed her kind humanity.

Florian's Omi, Maria, his Austrian grandmother, also gifted me with kindness and respect. I only met her once, during the first trip we took to Europe over a decade ago, after meeting Helen in Engelberg. In a small Austrian village, we spent the day with this remarkable woman who had lived through World War II and had many incredible stories to tell us, all narrated in her one and only language, German. She couldn't understand my language at all, and I couldn't understand hers, but that didn't mean we weren't understanding one another as human beings. I knew she accepted me from the moment I met her.

After we visited, Florian also made a call to Maria to tell her about our relationship. She told him, in German, "As long as you understand each other, that's the most important thing." That meant the world to Florian, to us. And she would continue to ask about me when he called her over the years before she passed away. The ability, demonstrated to me by Florian's grandmothers, to show respect and acceptance from a place of love is one of the inspiring forces behind my spiritual experience and my opening up to empathic connections with people. Some people lead with a love that seems spiritual and can transcend what prevents many from accepting others as they are.

MY TALE OF EMPATHY is a story of finding my spiritual self through my suffering, and through the many emotions and even love experienced by those around me. My suffering is not unlike your own. My faith and my belief in a higher power have only increased as I connect with the wholeness of myself as an empathic person. Instead of fighting the integral parts of myself—my depression, my empathy, and the emotional experiences that come with them—I want to accept all of it. I'm on a journey to expand my empathic connections with others, and this has started with accepting myself. I like to think that my empathy is a call from the cosmos and the stars above, informed by our shared humanity.

EIGHT

The Magic

WHEN I WAS LOST and suffering as a teenager, a handful of people in the media and their stories helped transport me away from my pain. I found a home where I could with Rosie O'Donnell, Ellen DeGeneres, and the popular culture representations of gay culture and gender expression. As a teen growing up in the late 1990s, there wasn't much representation of real queerness, and there were even fewer examples that I resonated with personally.

The Rosie O'Donnell Show broke ground for women in TV, and when she announced her lesbian identity it had a big impact in particular for people who were gay. She radiated an undeniable joy. I also sensed the emotion she had to hide, strategically, behind the broadcast. I would come home after being tormented at school, make myself something to eat, and sit down to watch her show. She took me away, if just momentarily, from the darkness in my life. Her one-hour show felt like a reprieve of sorts, a

heavenly feeling. Here was a gay woman on network television, strong and intelligent, sharing her love for unique
and eccentric people, and bringing joy to her audiences.
Rosie didn't come out until 2002, just months before the
end of her show, but I always found that her identity was
an unspoken part of her presence. At the beginning of each
episode, Rosie would literally reach out to her audience
to connect. This signalled a familiarity with isolation and
loneliness; she was someone who wanted to make it easier
for people like me to exist. It was a powerful gesture, a
human gesture. Her heart was open and available because
she made it that way.

The Rosie O'Donnell Show elevated examples of people
helping other people; it had the potential to change people's
lives, and it did so for many people like me. Her guests
ranged from celebrities and media personalities to activists
and change-makers. Some of these people were saving lives
by turning their interests into action; they were helping
people. Rosie used her celebrity and influence to shine a
light on important people, people who were working to
change the world in amazing ways. Her show ignited a
spark within me. It was more than an illusion on my TV
screen, it was the stuff of reality, of truth-telling. The stories of real people transmitted from her New York studio
to the tube-TV in my basement in Napanee inspired me.
Here were real people harnessing their power and passion
to reach out.

Ellen DeGeneres was another pioneer when both the
character she played in her sitcom and she herself came
out on national TV in 1997. Plastered on magazines and

newspapers and widely broadcast on television, Ellen's truth was impossible to ignore. Her coming out story demanded a bravery that touched me. It takes a tremendous amount of courage and insight to work through the script of heteronormativity, and even more, especially at that time, to be public about it. Ellen's success, her eventual self-actualization of her own truth and her sexuality, was a turning point in our culture in the recognition and representation of gay and lesbian people.

Rosie and Ellen were bright lights during my adolescence. Both were powerful and honest women daring to rewrite the heteronormative script that was constructed by those who monopolized cultural power in the media. The transformative and inspirational power of their effect on popular culture stuck with me. I learned about harnessing experience to make an impact. And this inspiring force became a powerful element in my own life.

THOUGH I WAS BORN into the home constructed for me — my body, my identity — throughout my life I have been deconstructed, reconstructed, and renewed by all the stories that hold truth for me. The stories of two people in particular embodied the magical humanity of our contemporary culture, how it resonates with us, and why it can make a significant difference in our lives.

My path crossed with that of a beloved figure of twentieth-century Western culture when I was still a child. She changed my life forever with a smile and a simple gesture.

On the morning of October 28, 1991, I woke up on the

edge of nervous excitement, and drove with my mom into Kingston from our home in Napanee. It was a crisp and sunny late-fall day, and the excitement in Kingston was palpable even to me at nine years old. I stood with my mom and some of her friends behind a barricade across from the Kingston Armouries, home to the Princess of Wales' Own Regiment. We were there to see the princess herself, Diana.

Would we catch a glimpse of her—the princess who had dared to break convention, who cared about alleviating human suffering, who was changing the world with a smile? The princess who had dramatically shifted the public perception of AIDS and brought awareness to the inhumane treatment of HIV patients when she shook the hand of a patient, flesh upon flesh. Diana elevated an empathy for people above all else. She was the princess of empathy, in my mind.

The public wasn't given access to the formal proceedings inside the Kingston Armouries that day, but we knew that she would have to exit the building in our direction at some point. When she finally did emerge from beyond the dark space of the doorway, she appeared like a sphere of light. I'm serious: it was *that* beautiful and majestic. Her luminosity seemed to make an entrance before she did.

I stood there on the other side of the road among hundreds of people who had amassed to see her and her royal husband, Charles, Prince of Wales. I was wearing my neon-green, blue, and purple winter parka and feeling slightly cold. But the warmth of her presence renewed my spirit. I had never before felt such a sense of loving admiration as when she walked out from the doorway and stood there in

crystal-clarity just a hundred feet away from us. She wore
a golden-yellow blazer with royal-blue buttons, a matching
skirt with a blue-gold rounded hat, and was surrounded by
her security escort along with handlers, publicists, and royal
assistants. I stood there transfixed, never turning my gaze,
with a hopeful and growing excitement. People around me
started to scream, calling her name over and over again. A
chanting choir of souls beckoned her closer.

The security detail and handlers began to steer her and
the Prince of Wales towards their car. I looked up at my
mom with wonder. "Will she come meet us, Mom?" I could
see the hesitation in my mom's eyes. She didn't want to
disappoint me. I had taken the day off school, and we had
travelled here from Napanee, hoping against hope that we
would meet the princess.

Suddenly, there was a commotion around Diana. I could
see her speaking with one of her handlers, and then she
broke ranks and proceeded to move in the direction of the
crowd of cheering fans. She had heard us calling for her.
She was moving towards us. A couple of her handlers tried
to stop her, but their efforts were futile. Diana was beyond
their control. She had learned to depart from formal structure to engage with the people who looked up to her and
appreciated her humanity. Her speed picked up a little as
she made her way across the road. Dozens of people followed close behind. This was obviously an unplanned part
of their day.

As she reached the barricade, Diana began to shake
hands and greet people in the crowd. She was less than
twenty feet away from me, and I started to get nervous.

"Mom, what should I tell her? What should I say?"

I could hear the building excitement in her shaky voice. "Tell her how you truly feel, Joshua."

I couldn't decide what to say. The light, her warmth, the love flowing so openly from her heart was my focus. Within a few minutes, she was less than five feet away from me. By this point, members of her security detail were gently nudging her along. She couldn't stop for every single person. But then she stopped right in front of me. Looking down, she smiled the most beautiful smile I had ever seen; it warmed my soul. I looked up at her. It was as though I could see her soul shining back at me. I reached out for her and her hand moved towards mine. The softness of her silk glove touched the bare flesh of my little hand. My heart was happy. I looked up into her eyes and the world around me stopped for a moment. I knew then exactly what I wanted to say to her: "You are beautiful, Princess Diana. You look like an angel."

Her smile widened and her eyes beamed. "Thank you so very much," she said to me as she held my hand. I felt so special in that moment. I know that she heard what I said. I mean, she really heard it and appreciated it. After all, it was from my little heart. I knew at that moment that she cared about me even though she didn't know me. She cared about me because I was a living, breathing human being in front of her. That was all that mattered. Being a human being was always enough for Princess Diana. She embodied love, she was the definition of love. Her smile will always stay with me.

Of course, in the early 1990s, not everyone had a camera

at their fingertips the way we do now and, sadly, we didn't get a photograph of me meeting her that day. But I didn't need a photo. I didn't need proof of that moment. My feelings were the proof. I knew our meeting would stay with me forever.

Then, at Christmas that year, I opened a gift and screamed with excitement. I couldn't believe what I held in my hands. Apparently, a few weeks before Christmas my mom had been contacted through her network of friends by a woman who had taken a photograph of a "young child shaking Princess Diana's hand" in Kingston. The photographer was trying to find the parents of this young child. My mom couldn't believe her luck—someone had taken a photo of that special moment after all! She framed it for me and wrote a message on the back about the magic of the experience. She also wrote a small column in Kingston's newspaper, *The Whig Standard*, discussing the impact of meeting Princess Diana and how that day had left us with such happiness and respect for the princess.

I stared deep into the photograph. I saw an angel of light and love meeting a young spirit for a reason, a spirit who was already being dehumanized and would come to face much pain, sorrow, and violence. Diana's beautiful smile shone down at me and left me with tangible magic, perhaps even protection. From that day on, I kept the photo of our meeting on my bedroom wall above me like a guardian angel. Each time I move, I hang the photo above me where I sleep.

I felt her tragic passing in 1997 with deep sadness and confusion. But I know that she will always exist in our collective memory; she will always be an angel who took time to be with us in physical form. She took time to be with me, to tell me that I mattered with the simple gesture of shaking my hand, thanking me, and smiling. Our paths crossed, ever so briefly, and her humanity has never left me.

And then there was another princess. I'm not joking when I say that in my house while I was growing up we probably watched the first three *Star Wars* films a hundred or more times. I was always intrigued by the films' sci-fi elements, but that wasn't the main reason I became such a huge fan of the series. For me, it was all about Princess Leia. And my admiration extended beyond that character into the very heart and soul of the woman who brought her to life: a feminist, a writer, an artist, a mother, a lover, a general, a queen, a fighter, and a force to be reckoned with — Carrie Fisher.

Carrie Fisher's unique gifts started to have a profound impact on me in my thirties. I devoured all of her memoirs and her fictional work. Her writing is open, lucid, dreamy, and direct. I laughed and cried, and my spirit soared while reading her words. She lived an unrivalled life. When she died in late 2016, I was absolutely gutted. I cried for days. She was unlike anyone else. She was Carrie, and she left a force with me that took time for me to unravel. Why had this legendary pop culture figure, writer, actor affected me so much? Why her?

I wrote a short piece for *HuffPost* shortly after her passing. I was in the bathtub crying during a depressed episode, and then I realized something powerful, yet so simple, while thinking about Carrie's words about mental illness: her contributions to popular culture had helped to make me feel less alone. I quickly dried off and ran to my laptop to write. I felt a calling to suddenly open up about my struggles with mental health. I had been suffering with dysthymia disorder, a consistent and moderate form of depression, for most of my life. I also wrote about the inextricable relationship that my mental illness has with my empathy. There are moments when I cannot distinguish my feelings from the feelings of others, a particularly challenging emotional experience when I already deal with depression. I went to Carrie for inspiration, for her stories, and for what she so courageously shared for so long in her public life and her writing. I ended up writing the piece in just a few hours and cited Carrie as my primary inspiration for opening up about my mental illness.

I then watched *Bright Lights: Starring Carrie Fisher and Debbie Reynolds*, the HBO documentary filmed before they both tragically passed, within days of each other, and I felt an even greater empathic pull to her spirit. I could see myself, my own confusing feelings between depression and empathy, my creative exhaustion and inspiration, and the darkness that seeps in and is impossible to control. In the film, she said that she'd always been an "open faced sandwich," emphasizing the awareness of her many layers exposed to the world despite the challenges she faced with bipolar disorder. Her playful, brilliant force beamed through the screen while I watched the documentary. I don't think there was a clear line for Carrie when it came to personal versus professional. The blurring of this boundary made her work very powerful, and I deeply resonate with the feeling of living a life without this clear distinction. She funnelled everything into her work. Even her tweets, mostly made up of emojis and symbols to spell words in cryptic construction, made sense to her because she saw from her own point of view.

Carrie was outspoken about experiencing bipolar disorder (like my mom) and she advised all who suffer with mental illness to seek support in community. The overwhelming response I received from readers of my *HuffPost* piece confirmed much of what she said: there are a great many people suffering in silence, waiting for someone to share similar experiences and to find commonality in their pain. Stigma in our society prevents us from sharing.

Carrie is the force that I follow for inspiration in how to engage with the public by being authentic while also retaining a sense of privacy. It's risky in general to share personal stories of mental illness, and especially risky when you are also trans, since many people believe, falsely, that being trans is in itself a mental illness. I will always look to Carrie's star burning bright in the cosmos for direction and inspiration, and to the words she left us in her books, while I engage with my own identity and the complicated relationship with representation in popular culture.

IN ADDITION TO the *Star Wars* saga, two films in particular stand out from my youth—films that allowed me to see parts of myself reflected on the screen: *To Wong Foo, Thanks for Everything! Julie Newmar* and *The Adventures of Priscilla, Queen of the Desert*. *Wong Foo* and *Priscilla* are films about the lives of drag queens, one set in the United States and the other in Australia. Both narratives revolve around road trips that take the drag queens on wild adventures. What influenced me in these films was the undeniable subversion of the gender binary, particularly in gender expression. Some of the characters in the films eventually come out as trans women, and some of the characters represent the playfulness of gender.

Drag, or gender as play, made me connect with these films. Believe me, there is a whole host of problems with both films in their representation of race, sexuality, and gender. But these issues aside, the representation of drag excited me as a teenager. There was a sense of freedom in the "cross-dressing" since it signalled something beyond the binary. I noticed, and felt comfort in, the representation of drag that highlights a continuum of gender presentation, and even identity, rather than an opposition between them.

Drag queens and kings have been some of the strongest pioneers in our community. They were at the forefront of significant moments in our history to agitate for necessary change and tolerance. In particular we remember the powerful action of drag queens of colour, trans people of colour, and gender-nonconforming people of colour at the Stonewall raid in 1969 in New York City. Drag queens formed a special part of my introduction to queer culture during my adolescence. When I was still underage, my friends and I visited the one gay bar that existed in Kingston, Ontario. There we found these incredible queens with their height, magical beauty, and strength of spirit, which both intimidated and intrigued me. The presence of drag queens often came with a dedication to telling a story about, or with, their bodies. They were in control of the space, commanding both from the identity underneath the makeup, clothes, and personas, but also from this very real place of sexuality, sex, and gender that results in drag. The films, and the drag queens represented in them, became a comfortable and welcoming part of the culture for me. Drag illuminated possibilities for gender to be malleable and fluid instead of static and fixed. These were the only examples of gender expression beyond the binary available to me. I have deep respect for drag culture in that it represents possibilities beyond what being assigned male or female tells us we have to be. Drag can enunciate something in between and beyond, opening a playfulness to explore and experiment—in essence, to be free and fluid.

It is interesting and apt that drag queens are contributing significantly to the visibility of non-binary identity and expression in today's popular culture. Historically, some drag queens have often been undermined, disrespected, and criticized for making a mockery of trans people in their performative plays of gender. Some members of the trans community broadly characterize drag as a disavowal of the validity of trans identity. Yes, there are some issues with drag, including the potential for misogyny and an insensitivity that can undermine trans identities, but this negative characterization bothers me. Drag cannot be homogenized. Drag enables a freedom to explore gender and to poke fun at the stereotypical performance of gender that we tend to always treat with serious fact in our lives. And its comedic effects loosen the suffocating grip that our culture has on gender.

The queens on the reality show, *RuPaul's Drag Race*, for instance, have been a gift to the popular culture discussion about gender beyond the binary because several of them — including Jinkx Monsoon, Violet Chachki, Adore Delano, Aja, Courtney Act, Shea Coulee, Kelly Mantle, and Sasha Velour — have come out as non-binary, genderfluid, or gender-nonconforming. Non-binary-identified drag queens defy the notion that all drag queens and kings are cis people. For instance, when Peppermint came out as a trans woman on the show, it created a ridiculous debate about whether or not drag queens can be trans and still perform drag. Ultimately, these drag queens are changing the script by dismantling the false notion that trans people, including non-binary people, aren't part of the drag community.

I honestly don't know why people are surprised. Of course, some drag queens are trans and non-binary! Their daily lives revolve around poking holes in the system of the gender binary by embodying, identifying with, and expressing new forms of gender. They highlight a growing cultural understanding that accepts gender as more of a fluid concept. These queens are at the forefront of our community. They are important forces who are boldly telling their stories and sharing their truths, stories that are not just welcome in the trans community but that have been a part of it all along.

• • •

DIANA AND CARRIE WERE unconventional in their own ways. Diana broke formation on that day to meet us, to meet me. Carrie openly shared a heavily stigmatized mental illness, created brilliant work, and was a powerful and inspirational force, despite some people thinking less of her because of her openness. She helped to deconstruct a societal view on mental health by showing that people with mental illness shouldn't be treated as less than human, as unstable and weak. They were both liminal forces, operating within and without convention, and that played a part in their ability to make a difference in people's lives. The princesses, Diana and Carrie Fisher, hold formative power in my life. They were real—stars made into flesh. They were magic.

Queens. Princesses. Hosts. Groundbreakers all. The magic of Diana, Carrie, Rosie, and Ellen opened up new realms that enabled me to see examples of powerful people breaking free from convention. The representation of drag, and the drag queens who are living authentically as they are, helped me to understand the validity of my own identity and expression, which I couldn't yet articulate in words. I found power in their magic to realize myself beyond the suffering.

NINE

The Geek

I WAS AN AVID READER as a child. My love of reading evolved into an enjoyment of Marvel comic books that resulted in a collection of thousands of comics still kept in a special place today. I preferred the stories of female characters: Silver Sable, Scarlet Witch, Invisible Woman, Rogue, and Storm. But first among these empowering superheroes was She-Hulk. She was the character I related to the most. Her strength came close to matching that of her cousin, Bruce Banner (The Hulk), and her day job was working as a lawyer. In some iterations of the title, She-Hulk breaks the fourth wall, acknowledging that she's a character within a comic book, and communicates directly with the reader. There is an in-betweenness to her place in the comic universe. She is both inside and outside the page. She embodies enormous physical and intellectual power, and she is autonomous, daring to criticize the presumed straight male reader gazing at her muscled green body — which was often hidden by only a small bathing suit — while she did physical battle with any number of foes. My love for She-Hulk opened me up to the power of created worlds to explore self-expression and identity. She-Hulk's gender expression, with her muscled body and physical prowess, was arguably non-normative for a female comic book character, particularly one created in 1980 — just two years before I was born.

I am a geek at heart. A non-binary geek — thankfully some parts of the geek culture are increasingly making efforts to be inclusive when it comes to trans, non-binary, and gender-nonconforming people. It surprises some people to know that I have thousands of comic books and that I'm an avid gamer. Those of us born in the early to mid 1980s were able to experience the dawning days of the internet in our adolescence, and growing up in front of the screen and on "the web" opened new worlds for my identity, which I was being forced to repress in reality.

When I was around eleven or twelve, I was able to connect with a creative part of myself and explore it with others from a safe distance. My parents bought our first family computer earlier than many other families in our neighbourhood, so we were one of the lucky families that used a dial-up connection to get the world's information at our fingertips. My parents imagined us enriching our education and knowledge by using it as a tool for schoolwork. They had no idea what it would expose me to.

As you can likely tell, for me and for many other social outcasts the internet in those early days was also a place to find people who seemed familiar and comfortable. It was a mystical place of wonder back then, an opportunity to communicate with other people who were similar by being different, before the emergence of social media. It was a kind of magic to be able to have a conversation with someone thousands of miles from where I was sitting in my basement in Napanee. I used the internet to explore bodies and sexuality (mostly by surreptitiously searching "male studs" and "male hunks," to the shock of my parents when they stumbled across my browser history), to further my gender exploration, and to ease my suffering by finding other people around the world who were like me.

My online social life began in chat rooms, where I casually communicated with people who were impossible to categorize based on age, race, gender, sex, or sexuality. Our identities were hidden behind the screen names and basic emojis. The chat rooms welcomed people trying to find connections to lessen their feelings of isolation, loneliness, and social marginalization. The chat communication was simple, nothing extraordinary, but I started yearning for the connection. Logging back into a room to see familiar names in the list on the right-hand side of the screen was exhilarating. This act of "logging in" became habitual, and it gave me a reprieve from my life. Enjoying this anonymous and free form of communication, I wanted to delve deeper into worlds that could, in different ways, take me away from my life in Napanee.

My chat conversations inspired the next stage of my virtual exploration: MMORPGs, or massively multiplayer online role-playing games. In the mid-1990s, MMORPGs were limited to a handful of games, certainly nothing like what is available today. MMORPGs are internet-based video games set in designed worlds with geographical boundaries containing multiple towns and cities, forests and mountains, temples and magic, and caves and dungeons for players to explore and become completely immersed in. These games connect players from around the world within a game world. The games enable communication and interaction between players, and they encourage players to join together to form partnerships and groups (often called guilds), which can result in long-term friendships. Sometimes these online relationships can evolve into real-life relationships when people get to know each other beyond the virtual world and their avatars.

Character creation is one of the most vital and exciting parts of playing an MMORPG. Whenever I started a new game, the character creation stage became therapeutic for me as I was able to create female-identified characters and manipulate their bodies and gender expressions in a way that I wasn't able to do with my own at the time. The first character I ever created was in a game called *Meridian 59*. This very early MMORPG was my first experience with virtual worlds, and while the graphics might now seem archaic, they weren't that far off from currently popular games like *Minecraft*. *Meridian 59* was a significant part of my life for many years. While I suffered in my real life, I found peace, friendship, and even magic in the game.

My first character was named Wintress. I had always been intrigued by tales of ice-themed sorceresses, isolated and alone in their sub-zero crystalline palaces, casting spells, summoning support, and fighting off intruders. So

I created a female-identified ice-sorceress with white hair
and a penchant for charming the players around her to protect me. Wintress swiftly developed a reputation as a leader
"in-game" (which refers to what exists in the game world).
I hid my real-life identity because I didn't think it would
harm the other players not to know who I was behind the
screen. Why should it matter anyway? I identified more with
being female than male at that time anyway, so Wintress
was more like the real me than I was able to be in reality.
It was incredibly empowering to step inside this artificial
world that felt so welcoming and real to me. *Meridian 59* was
a place of comfort to settle myself amidst the dehumanization happening in my real life on a daily basis at school.

After about a year or so playing as Wintress and forming
one of the strongest guilds inside the *Meridian 59* virtual
world on our server, I decided to tell my fellow guild mates
and friends that I wasn't actually female behind the screen.
At that time, there were a few members of my guild whose
innocuous flirting had turned into requests to know more
about the real me. I felt it was time to tell them that I was
really a teenage boy — a narrative enforced upon me by my
tormentors at school. Obviously I was not an ice-sorceress
slaying characters with my dark magic and my guild mates,
but I was not a girl, either. Most of my in-game friends took
the news about my "real" identity well. I was relieved that
they knew who I was behind the screen, although it felt as
though Wintress was part of me too, which I believe is an
early articulation of my non-binary identity and expression. I was both Josh and Wintress, my identity forged by
both realities.

I started playing another MMORPG named *The Realm Online*. This game was more community based than *Meridian 59*. I became involved with a guild in *The Realm Online* that foregrounded our culture's absolute fixation with technology. The guild was called MECH. Members of the guild had to shed their fleshly human identities in-game by adopting a cyborg-like character that served the guild's mandate. The adoption of the MECH title even came with a regimented form of communication. I role-played as MECHNorth for more than a year in-game. The guild's members were actually quite diverse, even if we all celebrated homogeneity in our behaviour and communication. I started to realize that other players preferred to be absolved of their fleshly life while in-game because, like me, they needed an escape. I developed relationships with some of these players, some of which became romantic and continued outside of the game. Our real-life identities were known to each other. While playing *The Realm Online*, I was involved in a queer relationship in-game while playing as a cyborg who was supposed to be stripped free of all human emotions — yet there I was engaging, quite deeply and profoundly, in a beautiful and humane experience by role-playing in a way that felt more like playing who I was all along.

From age fourteen until my early twenties, these virtual worlds — *Meridian 59*, *The Realm Online*, and then *World of Warcraft* — opened up safe spaces for me to explore who I was without the risk of being attacked or assaulted in real life. Playing online and offline role-playing video games (RPGs) was a form of therapy for me throughout my adolescence. The offline RPGs had fantasy-scapes with diverse characters and rich storylines that completely immersed me and helped distance me from the nightmarish reality that greeted me outside their confines.

I could never have imagined in my adolescence the impact that these video games would come to make on our culture. The effect of these games on players' lives transcends the screen-spaces. The game worlds found in both BioWare's *Dragon Age* and *Mass Effect* games and Bethesda's *Fallout* and *Elder Scrolls* games contain rich and diverse representations of sex, gender, sexuality, and race. You are able to create an almost lifelike character before you immerse yourself in hundreds of hours of narrative-driven game play. The games contain countless choices that have a wide-ranging impact on the story, and non player characters (NPCs, controlled by the game's intelligence and designed by writers and artists, independent from a human player) with whom you can develop both friendly and romantic relationships.

The option to have romantic relationships with non-player characters is a beautiful new feature introduced within the last decades to role-playing video games. You can choose to have heterosexual, gay, lesbian, bisexual and queer romantic relationships in-game with non-player characters. The player develops feelings, attachments, and emotional responses to affecting streams of experience in-game, which change depending on the choices that are made and how the player feels about the beautifully written NPCs that play a vital role in the main and side quests. In particular, *Dragon Age Inquisition* (the third game in this specific BioWare franchise) introduced a trans male character named Krem who comes with a brief storyline, authentically written, about his experience as a trans person within the game world of Thedas.

The evolution of these games will hopefully introduce non-binary characters and gender-neutral pronouns so that players can freely explore their gender identity. For the most part, the mainstream RPGs—like the *Dragon Age, Elder Scrolls*, and *Mass Effect* franchises, and even late 2018's *Assassin's Creed Odyssey* (venturing into RPG territory)—provide two gender options for characters: male or female. I now feel incredibly conflicted choosing between one or the other, so although it would create work for the teams behind these games, creating a gender-diverse pathway for some players to take would reflect the reality of some of us who have a hard time making a binary choice. Nevertheless, I still feel empowered by instilling in the character, either male or female, my own feelings about their gender expression and identity by modifying their outfits, armour, hair, and makeup to reflect my own identity. The future promises an opportunity for people to be able to play with gender in these safe virtual spaces, both online and offline.

In my journals as a teenager, I often wrote with concern about my "addiction" to video games. I think that this concern stemmed from my parents' constant worry that these games would distract me too much from reality, and that I spent an unhealthy amount of time playing rather than living. But I was living my way safely. Thank the goddess for these games. I needed these games to help me survive. I still need them to retreat from the pressures of life. They contain expansive universes beyond my limited world, or the world that we're supposed to just accept. In my youth, I could barely breathe in my real-life world. I couldn't exist as I was. I lost touch with myself, but these video games helped me find space away from the trauma of being bullied for years, and they helped me retain a connection to who I truly was, even if it meant that I had to role-play that identity for decades in virtual spaces before I was able to live it.

TEN

The Filmmaker

MY PARENTS HAD HIGH hopes for my career. I was a pre-cocious child in their eyes. My early success in elemen-tary school created the expectation that I would pursue a career as a doctor, lawyer, or some other white-collar professional. I was enrolled in "gifted" studies during ele-mentary school and the first year of high school, before the chaos of bullying consumed me and destroyed my ability to focus on schoolwork. I always felt uncomfortable with the alienating effect of studying a year above most of my other classmates, although I could share the experience with my best friend Kristin since she was also placed in the "gifted" program. In addition to being different, I was also "gifted"; it was like a second stamp of the outcast that I had to bear. And my "gifted" status brought with it significant pressure from family members and teachers. Once the bar of expectation is set, it's difficult to change what people believe you can accomplish. The pressure was overwhelming, especially when my grades started to plummet at the end of grade nine.

It took time to get myself back to a space of academic concentration. After completing high school, I took two years off before beginning my post-secondary education at Algonquin College in Ottawa. My dad and I discussed my future career options many times when I was in my early twenties. He never gave up on the potential that he saw in me. His high expectations were both a gift and an enormous pressure. Both my parents had undergraduate degrees and they insisted on a higher education for me. With these high expectations, and my own interest in asking questions, I embarked on an academic path that eventually resulted in my doctoral degree.

One day in particular stands out as the point at which I came to recognize my career path as a filmmaker and writer. I was in my early twenties, living with my dad, sitting in front of a dark television screen in our living room. As I sat there, staring into the space beyond, my dad, behind me in his chair, was boring me with the same old script: "Joshua, you have to figure out your life. You are in your early twenties now. You're an adult, and you have so much potential. You can't waste it by just playing video games and working at Le Chateau."

I blocked out his words and started to disassociate from hearing the same thing a million times. I disassociated often as a form of self-protection against the pressures that descended on me. I could feel my mind drifting into the black space that held my partial reflection as he tried to encourage me. Something within me clicked in that moment. I will always remember what came next.

All the possibilities from the last decade of soaking up stories in this magical screen suddenly came to light. I knew at that moment what I needed to do with my life. I had connected with my dream—not a dream in a defined sense, but my own reality that I knew would fulfill my life's purpose. I came back to myself from my trance.

"I know what I want to do!" I could feel my dad's growing curiosity behind me, but I continued to stare into the television. "I want to change people's lives through the media."

It felt so good to say it. Perhaps I had been feeling this passion for artistic action since my adolescence, growing up in a household with parents who appreciated film and television and the ways entertainment can alleviate suffering through simultaneous escape and self-exploration.

"I want to save lives, to make a difference, Dad," I said excitedly. Nervously I turned to him, unsure how he would respond. Thankfully, he encouraged me to follow my dream wherever it might take me. I think there was a part of him that was simply relieved to finally hear something from me about a career—any career, really—beyond the retail sales work I was doing at the time. At least now I had expressed a clear objective.

But how realistic was this dream to change people's lives through the media, through this magical screen that had deeply affected my own life and taken me away from so much pain? I knew that it was a long shot. I mean, how would someone from the small town of Napanee break into that enormous and intimidating industry? My goal seemed unattainable at the time, but that didn't stop me. I completed a one-year introductory Arts, Culture, and Media program at Algonquin College, where I learned some of the skills needed to create my own forms of representation, and, more importantly, reactivated my academic focus. For the first time, the picture of my dreams took shape. The fire for learning about myself, and how to effect change, was just beginning.

My dream of making a difference with my life and art entered a new phase the following year at Western University. I moved to the London, Ontario, campus and enrolled in an Introduction to Film Studies course. My professor, Dr. Barbara Bruce, became a brilliant force in my life that year. By a sort of magical coincidence, she is the sister of acclaimed queer Canadian artist and filmmaker Bruce LaBruce, whose films break ground for queer representation. Dr. Bruce stood tall in her own intellectual capacity beyond any teacher I'd had before her. Her love for film was conveyed to a class of over a hundred students — some eager, some tired, and some sincerely curious, like me and Florian, who was also enrolled in the class. She was a beacon for those of us who were truly passionate about film.

Dr. Bruce's comparative analysis of *The Wizard of Oz* and *Star Wars*, within the context of parallels and post-modern pastiche, was a special awakening for me. She peeled off the illusionary layers of both films to reveal the methods, the artistic elements, and the intertextual influences that inspired their creators and their stories. I had been watching films completely blind to the mechanisms that make these giant stories so affective for human beings. Dr. Bruce revealed to me cinema's machinations: complex and carefully constructed illusions, sometimes crafted with a care in mind to change people's lives.

Dr. Chika Kinoshita was another film studies professor at Western University who expanded my worldview with her courses on Japanese cinema. Her brilliantly woven lectures on samurai films, in particular Oshima Nagisa's *Gohatto* (about queer love in the samurai class), presented with important historical and cultural context, made me realize the importance of acknowledging the specificity of sex, gender, and sexuality, and how these terms differ greatly from one culture to the next. Dr. Kinoshita taught me that our understanding should shift with cultural frameworks and cultural history—the importance of time and place.

In Dr. Kinoshita's course I began to analyze cinematic representations of gender and sexuality within the context of Japan's rich and diverse cultural history. Her lessons compelled me to study further under her guidance in my undergraduate work, and then in my research at UBC under Dr. Sharalyn Orbaugh towards my M.A., resulting in a Social Sciences and Humanities Research Council–sponsored trip to Japan and my thesis "Queer Japanese Cinema."

The next step of my artistic awakening combined this critical analysis of film with my own growing awareness of my identity, in terms of both my sexuality and my gender. My second year at Western, when I was twenty-five, will remain one of the most important times of my life, because this was the moment when I started to reconnect with the part of myself from childhood that I had lost during my adolescence, and it was thanks to two remarkable people in particular: Dr. Susan Knabe and Dr. Wendy Gay Pearson. Susan and Wendy are now dear friends. They have been together as partners for decades. They attended my wedding to Florian. They hold their hearts close in their teaching. Their guidance vanquished many illusory subjective components of myself that I had been holding on to. They believed in me and they invested in me. They helped me get back to myself.

I first met Susan in her Women's Studies office on a chilly and rainy fall day with a page of notes on my clipboard, eagerly seeking direction for the evolution of my undergraduate studies. Susan spent more than an hour with me. She saw something in me, and she helped to shift my focus to what she obviously gleaned was a personal exploration yet to come through my academic work. Her guidance connected me to her partner, Wendy, who thankfully had a position in the Department of Film Studies. Wendy saw the light hiding deep within me, my spirit that was lost to me and twisted. She took my inner light in her hands, breathed brilliance into me, and aided the end of the slumber of my suffering. My experience at Western, with Wendy mentoring me, was truly that powerful.

Wendy taught a Film Studies course on representations of gender and sexuality in cinema. It remains the most important and formative educational experience of my life. I started to see my own world, what felt honest to me, reflected in film. It was a time when my self, past and present, began to align and make sense. We studied early examples of queer and trans representation from different cinematic periods and world cinemas. Wendy's lectures elegantly delivered rich analysis bolstered by a range of theoretical lines of inquiry. My personal favourite was critical theory, in which we learned about the censorship of queer and trans lives in cinema; biological and cultural constructions of sex, gender, and sexuality; and the emergence of new queer cinema through the works of John Greyson, Tom Kalin, Todd Haynes, and producer Christine Vachon. I realized that dominant voices and creators — typically white, heterosexual, cis men — had held the reins of mainstream cinema for too long, and how marginalized voices disrupt forms of representation by intervening with new stories, which are then silenced by an industry that refuses to address the shifting reality of society.

At the heart of Wendy's teaching was the acknowledgement of cultural specificity for gender and sexuality. Being taught how sex, gender, and even sexuality shifts with time and place excited me. I gave a presentation in the class on two films that represented gender-fluidity in childhood, the Filipino film *The Blossoming of Maximo Oliveros* and the French film *Ma Vie en Rose*. I didn't realize it at the time, but I was drawn towards these two films because the fictional stories of the two assigned-male-at-birth protagonists shared a special connection to my own truth. My presentation, entitled "Gender Identity Transcendence: A Rainbow of Possibilities," was the spark behind the central academic query later explored in my doctoral dissertation: Why do we think about gender as only two, and why is the media a form of constructed reality that we endow with truth in spite of its oversimplification of a complex reality?

I became fascinated with the possibility of the illusory media-scapes created by the artists' positionality and identity. I wanted to know more about storytelling in this cinematic realm—how do artists intervene and make change through this powerful artistic medium? And how could I enact change in cinema through my own forms of creation?

I also learned about the burden of representation for queer and trans filmmakers, producers, and actors who defy conventional forms of representation to tell new stories. Representation becomes the main vehicle for delivery and, unfortunately, it is often elevated to the platform of singularity, where one representation becomes the example for all. The person who creates, or who is represented, is thus responsible for representing the entire group. This is a real problem, considering that even within a group of people under one identity there exists a multiplicity of difference. People want figures of popular culture to tell a story that can be easily understood and categorized, so that these stories make sense to all of us, but the real picture of humanity isn't so simple. So, we understand one story to be the one and only story for all trans people, or all queer people, or all people of colour. This is called burden of representation, and it places an enormous amount of pressure on the individual: one person should never hold responsibility for an entire group of people. But it does show the enormous impact that a single artist can make.

We let our guard down to be entertained by media; we become comfortable with the manufactured screens that deliver these stories in the visual realm. When the viewer is vulnerable, media can make interventions and impact lives that otherwise seem closed or intolerant towards difference. Fear can be transformed into acceptance and understanding as we are entertained, experiencing the habitual enjoyment we receive from watching and listening. We let go in a leisurely manner and open up through the act of media consumption. It is pleasurable and it provokes.

In the later stages of my undergraduate work at Western, I started to think seriously about how to bring marginalized and otherwise invisible stories to light through my future work as a filmmaker. I thought about the risks that I could take with film to tell new stories that may or may not incite an intervention, that could make a significant impact on society. With several of my friends I formed Standing Against Queer Discrimination (SAQD), a student activist organization initially conceived to advocate against the Canadian Blood Services ban on blood donations from men who have sex with men (MSM). This led to the creation of Western University's first queer film festival, Emergence, dedicated to uplifting queer and trans stories from the point of view of academics and artists. Emergence received extensive funding from several faculties, departments, and organizations at Western. We successfully invited prominent queer filmmakers John Greyson and Tom Kalin to give keynote presentations, and we screened a wide range of domestic and foreign queer and trans cinema. Emergence was, in large part, inspired and supported by Wendy's and Susan's unique approach to teaching, and the supportive space they offered their students. Emergence has taken place annually at Western for the past ten years. It stands as a legacy for our group of friends—Florian, Laura, Gregory, Anjeet, Mel, Emily, Wendy, and Susan—and is something we can all be proud of.

AFTER GRADUATING IN 2009, Florian and I moved to Vancouver to be close to a thriving film industry and to turn our passion into practice. For him, this meant starting as a production assistant in the locations department on a big Hollywood feature film while I started my Master of Arts Film Studies program at UBC. A few years later in Vancouver, we formed our production company, Turbid Lake Pictures. Our specific goal with TLP was to tell cinematic stories that make a positive difference in people's lives and contribute to a shift in the culture for LGBTQ representation. After taking our first few years in the city to put down roots in the film industry, we made three short films together and a feature-length documentary; our most recent film, *Henry's Heart*, was shot in June 2018.

Our first film, a short entitled *Whispers of Life* (2013), told the fictional story of a gay teen who faces bullying and considers suicide. The narrative elevates the vital story of suicide prevention by imagining the impact of a single open and honest conversation. The original screenplay, written by Florian, was partly inspired by my own experiences with bullying and with losing someone close to suicide—someone I had shared intimacy with during my early twenties, before I met Florian. The inclusion of these personal elements wasn't entirely intentional. I've had people tell me that our lead character, played by Travis Nelson, resembles me, especially in the contributions made by our costume designer, makeup artist, and hairstylist. Personally, I don't see the resemblance when I watch the film, but I understand why some people might feel this way. What we experience in our own lives as artists always seems to inform artistic creation. It is all subjective, after all.

Part of the inspiration for Tom's character was Gabriel (not his real name, but I'll use this angelic name to protect his family's privacy), who came from across the Ottawa River in Gatineau, Quebec. Gabriel and I dated for a couple of months in my early twenties — this was shortly after I almost lost my life to the hate crime in Kingston. Gabriel was a loving and caring soul who found success at a young age in his career with a major car manufacturer. Our relationship ended prematurely because we weren't on the same page romantically. I wasn't ready for a long-term relationship, and I wasn't ready to reciprocate his expression of love for me.

We didn't communicate for months after our relationship ended. Then one day, Gabriel reached out to me in an email. He missed me, and wanted to connect with me again. I stared at the computer screen, reading his email over and over again, his words punctuated by bat and heart emojis, and a mix of upper- and lowercase letters. I just couldn't bring myself to send him a response. It was clear from his email that he still cared for me, but I couldn't let him think that I still cared for him that way. I didn't want to lead him on. I decided not to respond to his email. Perhaps I should have, if only out of friendship. But I didn't. And that decision will always haunt me.

A few weeks later, I received a call from a mutual friend, who had dated Gabriel a couple of years before me. The call came at night, and I could tell right away that something was seriously wrong. He told me that Gabriel had died by suicide. He had been found in his garage. A nightmare of emotions hit me. I fell to my knees and began to sob. How could I have been so heartless as to ignore his email? Was I partly to blame? I stumbled downstairs in a fit of emotions and woke up my dad. He held me while I just cried uncontrollably in his arms.

I had never lost someone to suicide before. There were so many unanswered questions, and so much pain. Poor, sweet Gabriel, with his soft lips and warm heart. I would never hear his kind voice with his thick French accent ever again. I couldn't believe that his death was real. I didn't want to accept it. It all felt like some sort of sick joke.

Gabriel's funeral was open casket. I will never forget the cold, empty feeling that pulsed through my body and my spirit when I saw him lying in the funeral home. An overwhelming energy of sorrow soaked the entire space. The room was cold, and dimly lit with a few candles and soft lights. The depth of grief that poured out, energetically and verbally, from Gabriel's parents and siblings made me disassociate from the service. I walked up to his casket and was stunned by the sudden reality. What remained there in front of me was only a physical shell. It wasn't a joke; Gabriel was gone.

For years, I felt a tremendous guilt for ignoring his attempt to reach out to me. Now I know that it wasn't my fault. Suicide is no one's fault. It also isn't about us, the survivors. It is about the person who died. We need to focus on the people who need us. We need to communicate more and talk openly about suicide.

Whispers of Life was intended as an intervention on behalf of suicide prevention, particularly the epidemic of suicide among queer and trans youth. Queer and trans youth face increased rates of suicidal ideation due to bullying, alienation from family and friends, and the realities of homophobia and transphobia that are present in our society. The film was my contribution to the important discussions we need to have within our communities on this subject. *Whispers of Life* screened at film festivals all over the world, and won multiple awards.

Anyone who works in film can appreciate how difficult it is raise funds when you don't have a demo reel and can't apply for private or public grants (most of these grants require a filmmaker to have screened at least one film at a festival). In making *Whispers of Life*, we found our angel-champion Rosemarie A. Delgado, an incredible human being from the Philippines who supported the project financially. Additionally, we relied on the generosity of strangers, crowdfunding from hundreds of people online who believed in the project and wanted to see it made. The film was then distributed across Canada to elementary schools, high schools, colleges, and universities, with over two hundred copies sold to the institutional market. *Whispers of Life* also took Florian and me on a screening tour to the Philippines, supported by Rose and one of my kind faculty advisers at the University of British Columbia, Dr. Leonora A. Angeles. We screened the film to thousands of students at several institutions in the Philippines. It was pure magic to see the reaction on the faces of kids and teens who watched our little film. I know that we have contributed, in a small part, to the conversation about suicide prevention, particularly as it relates to anti-queer bullying and LGBTQ youth.

LIMINA (2016), OUR NEXT SHORT FILM, reflected my life experience as a gender-nonconforming person more accurately than *Whispers of Life*. The film's fictional story, again written by Florian, is about a young gender-creative child who touches the lives of their fellow townspeople with the kindness of their heart. The central character, Alessandra (played by Ameko Eks Mass Carroll), focuses their kindness on a young woman named Maria (played by Chelsey Reist) who is mourning the loss of her small child. *Limina* expresses important themes of respect, appreciation, and love for gender-creative and trans youth, rather than focusing on hatred and intolerance. We wanted to inject a positive and lighthearted representation of a trans kid into a cinematic landscape otherwise dominated by tragic and dark representation.

We turned again to crowdfunding, and our angel-champion Rose, to raise the film's budget. With a slightly higher budget in hand than we had for *Whispers of Life*, we started to discuss where we could shoot *Limina*, away from the familiar locations in Vancouver, to make it a more unique visual experience and to tap into Florian's cultural background. Florian's Swiss heritage infused the original script of *Limina* with fresh and exciting possibilities for new settings, so we decided to explore shooting the film in Switzerland, in Ticino, the country's Italian-influenced region.

We travelled to Switzerland in the summer of 2015 and began working with Ticino's Film Commission to explore potential locations and interview possible crew members. We even met with some cinematographers and casting directors in Zurich, and with public officials to determine if there would be interest in funding for the film, considering its unique subject matter and the combination of our cultural backgrounds and experience. Our dream of shooting this beautiful story of a gender-creative child in the magical landscapes of Ticino seemed within reach.

Around this time, the Swiss media began reporting on the story of us travelling from Vancouver to Switzerland to shoot the film. The *Obwaldner Zeitung*, the main newspaper in the canton where Florian grew up, featured him as their "person of the month" with a big headline and a picture of us in front of Eugenisee, the lake named after Florian's great-great grandfather, Eugen Hess, in Engelberg. Of course, we knew that their feature would also focus on the fact that Florian was a Swiss cis man in a queer relationship with a Canadian trans person. However, what we didn't foresee was that the limitations of the Swiss-German language meant that I was described as a "transsexual" in the article, not non-binary, and *Limina*'s story was said to be about a "transsexual" rather than a gender-creative child.

The visibility of the project in the media caught the attention of an extremist anti-LGBTQ and anti-Semitic group in Europe. They responded to the film's subject matter by creating a petition that employed transphobic rhetoric fuelled by an archaic perspective on trans people. The petition claimed that we were travelling to Switzerland with "Western LGBTQ lobby" interests to pervert Swiss and European children and indoctrinate them into the evils of transsexual ideology. It was clearly written by people who were also misogynistic, deeply racist, and altogether homophobic and transphobic. Their goal was to appeal to the Swiss cantons (similar to provinces or states) of Obwalden and Nidwalden to stop potential public funding for the film. They claimed that we were planning to damage and brainwash the minds of Swiss children by perverting the classic Swiss children's tale *Heidi* with our genderfluid version. Of course, *Limina* is nothing like *Heidi*, and it was never our intention to make a genderfluid version of anything—*Limina* was a completely original idea! Needless to say, this hateful characterization of our film and the petition against it was surreal and disturbing, and at the same time highlighted the reason for the film in the first place.

The petition against *Limina* is an example of the censorship and vitriol that a trans artist—any public trans person, really—faces every day. It condemned all trans people in sweeping terms, and made the retrogressive and dangerous claim that trans people are mentally ill, which flies in the face of the widely accepted position of the World Professional Association of Transgender Health (WPATH). On a personal level, I was called a "spawn of Satan," among other expletives.

The transphobic attack on our little film resulted in serious pressure being placed on the public officials in

Obwalden and Nidwalden. We became concerned that the criticism would scare the committees and officials who adjudicate applications into acting against our funding applications. And yet, *Limina*'s subject matter was welcomed by many established and notable organizations in Canada and Switzerland. Canada's oldest transgender organization stated, "We at Gender Mosaic wish to denounce any petition or action that seeks to block or hinder the *Limina* film project." Gender Creative Kids Canada said, "Gender identity is naturally occurring in all human beings and develops in early childhood. Gender Creative Kids Canada supports film productions that represent a broad range of gender identities in children and young people." Transgender Network Switzerland (TGNS) expressly distanced itself from the petition and welcomed the aims of *Limina*. TGNS president Henry Hohmann stated, "Children, in particular trans youth, have the right to live their gender. Information of parents and schools, but also the visibility of trans children in our society is one of our key concerns." And Dr. Cecilia Dehjne, one of the authors of the 2011 Swedish study cited by the petition, stated that "this petition incorrectly uses our research to attempt to prove that gender confirmation surgery increases the suicide rate for trans people. I denounce this petition's dangerous and misguided use of our research and this misuse is what actually could harm trans people and by that increase the risk of suicide."

In response to the personal and professional attacks, Florian and I publicly explained that the collective's intent to influence government funding bodies in order to silence our film only served to validate the importance of a film like *Limina*. We emphasized that our film would highlight the role of parental support, acceptance, and appreciation of trans youth, and was grounded in the awareness of accepting gender-creative children. The tactics employed to censor our film proved that transphobic people see a world that is changing. The rise of what they call the "LGBTQ Lobby" and "Gender Lobby" unhinges the mechanisms of power that are at the foundation of their attempts to colonize and indoctrinate based on a Eurocentric patriarchal system of power. *Limina* was to be a work of art imbued with empathy and kindness to challenge fear, intolerance, and hatred through an articulation of humanity, and serious attempts were being made to prevent our artistic expression.

I received a direct message on Twitter from a young person during the backlash. This person described how their father was against our film and had signed the petition to censor it. I moved the conversation to private to seek additional information as I wondered why this young person was reaching out to me. They explained that their father was "very religious" and intolerant of the LGBTQ community. They responded by saying that they were looking forward to the film and praised us as an inspirational force in their life. They wanted us to continue to spread our message of acceptance and love.

Amidst the difficult process of dealing with the hatred and fear directed at us, here was this young person clearly coping with their own identity and how it related to their family dynamic, reaching out to me to show kindness and appreciation. This moment fed into our determination to make the film. Here was an example of our film's message already reaching beyond bigotry and religious dogma to a new generation who wanted to move forward with accepting people as they are. It validated how art can act as a cultural intervention, and it helped me to focus on the kind message that can overshadow the hateful ones stemming from fear.

We decided to film *Limina* in Vancouver after all. As we feared, the Swiss cantons rejected our applications for funding, and without their support we couldn't afford to make the film in another country on our limited budget. So we found a location in Vancouver that suited our vision of a small Swiss village and shot the film with an amazing Vancouver-based cast and crew. *Limina* screened all over the world at two dozen film festivals, and then it made history in a big way for non-binary visibility, awareness, and recognition.

The young performer who played the role of Alessandra, Ameko Eks Mass Carroll, identifies as genderfluid (under the non-binary umbrella). Ameko, who uses he/him/his pronouns, expressed his gender across a spectrum when we auditioned him for the part, but we didn't ask for his identity during the audition or when we cast him. It was during filming that Ameko's mother told us that he seemed genderfluid growing up. Ameko had told her that some days he felt like a girl and other days like a boy, and some days both. It was indeed a powerful coincidence that we had managed to cast a genderfluid performer in the role of Alessandra.

When we finished the film, we submitted it for consideration to the Leo Awards, British Columbia's annual awards competition for the film and television industry. A few months prior, non-binary-identified actor Kelly Mantle had made history in the United States by becoming the first performer to be eligible for both the male and female award categories at the Academy Awards. This decision made international headlines and inspired our own submission to the Leos. Florian and I decided to take a chance and appeal to the Leo Awards to accept Ameko's submission in both the male and female categories for best performance in a short film, since Ameko told us clearly during shooting that he doesn't exclusively identify as a boy or a girl. At the time, the Leo Awards only allowed each performer to be categorized as either male or female. I thought, since the Academy Awards did it, why shouldn't other organizations around the world follow suit? The system of categorizing performers into male and female seemed arbitrary and archaic to me. I was interested to find out that at one time there was only one category for performers at the major film and TV award competitions, and women in the industry had to agitate for their own category because men were unfairly dominating. I understand the importance of this inclusion, but now that we are finally starting to recognize gender beyond just male and female, we need to make another shift to recognize members of the industry both in front of and behind the camera with their own identities, which might be neither male nor female.

After learning that Ameko wouldn't feel comfortable being identified with either the male or female category, we sent an appeal to the Leo Awards to consider our request, with the earnest approval of Ameko and his mother.

It would mean a big policy change if they accepted our request, but the Academy Awards had already made the shift with my friend Kelly Mantle, so there was a precedent. The Leo Awards eventually responded with a positive result. They agreed to our request to accept Ameko's submission under both male and female performer categories. The decision made international news, with *The Hollywood Reporter* writing an exclusive and over thirty national and international newspapers following their lead. It was a historic moment for trans inclusivity in the film industry in Canada and beyond. It was also a moment to recognize that we all need to work towards creating a more accepting society. Achieving equality is not just a matter of making everything fifty-fifty—we need to also recognize people who don't fit within this binary framework. *Limina* inspired productive conversations and signalled a shift in the film industry that will hopefully be followed up with more examples of industry members speaking out and tangible action to include more non-binary voices, characters, and stories in both film and television.

OUR LATEST PROJECT, *Henry's Heart* (2019), is our last short film before we begin focusing on full-length features. *Henry's Heart* continues our creative quest as filmmakers to challenge under-representation. This time, we focused not just on representing queer sexuality but also on including Indigenous characters to reclaim some of the lost history of Indigenous soldiers who fought on the side of Canada in many wars—particularly for our film, in the Korean War.

Our cast and crew included Indigenous people, and on our production team we included an Indigenous associate producer who also acted as our Indigenous consultant for the production. Henry wasn't initially written as an Indigenous character, but we ended up casting the magnificent Lorne Cardinal in the role, with the help of our casting director Candice Elzinga, so two of our four characters are Indigenous. We had previously worked with Lorne when he played a supporting role in *Limina*. We recognized his gift for storytelling, and it was the missing piece.

This casting made for a powerful romantic connection between Henry, a Cree character played by a Cree actor, and Walker, a Musqueam character played by a Musqueam actor by the name of Malcolm Sparrow-Crawford, who happens to be the nephew of Leona M. Sparrow (Director of Treaty, Lands, and Resources for the Musqueam Indian Band). While shooting a special scene in the film in which the two characters lovingly embrace, my friend and our associate producer and Indigenous consultant Jules Arita Koostachin looked at me with tears in her eyes (something I've rarely seen), smiled, and nodded her head before giving me a warm hug signalling that we were paying respect with our story. As white settlers, we can't claim that *Henry's Heart* is an Indigenous story, but it does have a narrative that centres around a fictional story of the love found between these two Indigenous characters who meet each other during the horrors of war, a love that stands the test of time and will, we hope, be inspiring for viewers around the world.

Henry's Heart's timeless love story elevates the power of nostalgia and memory. The representation of queer sexuality is intrinsic to the world within the film and reflects our own reality as filmmakers without a need for explanation.

Diversity has become a buzzword in the film and television industry, though there is still a significant gap between the idea and a widespread authentic move towards representing our human reality. The promise of diversity to challenge under-representation will fail if media continue to rely on common tropes, formulaic and archetypical, rather than the wide and varied set of truths that many of us live. Media should reflect the reality of society. We are in a watershed moment for trans representation and inclusivity in the film industry. I know from experience that major studios want to involve trans people, including non-binary people, when telling our stories. But I think these studios are still trying to figure out *how* to include us in a way that would transcend the monolithic portrayal that ends up serving as the one and only representation. Studios need to hire the people whose stories they want to tell. They need to involve us, cast us, and consult with us.

My interventions with my filmmaking have evolved from intentional, explicit representation to representing the reality of diversity for what it is—a powerful maturation that parallels my life as a person who understands the incredible power art can have as an agent of change.

ELEVEN

The Advocate

OVER THE NINE YEARS of my university studies, my experience of academia evolved. I developed an affinity for putting theory into practice by not only acting to reclaim myself, but working to assist people like me with my advocacy. Fighting the cultural schema of the gender binary was one such instance. Through my doctoral research at the University of British Columbia, I found the tools to carve out clarity about my complex trans identity, sharpening my voice as an advocate. What ignited from my research was an intimate path of learning to come to terms with my own language. I was able to do this subjective mining by first recognizing and then challenging a dominant idea that I termed the "transgender metanarrative"—the dominant understanding in society that most trans people are either men or women. *Transgender* referring to being a woman or man makes sense for many trans people, but it didn't make sense for me. Consider it for a second: when you think about trans people, do the trans people that come to mind identify as trans men and trans women? This understanding is expanding as non-binary visibility widens, and I'm certainly not suggesting that our language shouldn't elevate all trans lives, including trans men and trans women. This is especially important considering that much focus needs to be given to the lives of trans women, particularly trans women of colour, who have to face a high risk of violence in our society caused by the intersecting oppressions of race, sex, and gender. But the dominant narrative I was hearing about in the media made me think that there might be only one possible way for me to be a trans person.

Was I a trans woman? Why didn't I feel comfortable with that identity at the time? Coming to terms with the fact that I am neither a man nor a woman was a part of my process of rediscovering myself. I knew that I was not happy as a man or a woman, so something had to change. I thought that this change had to match what I knew about trans people through popular culture, and back in 2013–14 I wasn't seeing anyone like me; there was a decided absence of non-binary trans people who were public with their identities.

I had to come to terms with my non-binary identity. What I mean is that I finally found the language to describe me, that felt like home to me. I had always felt non-binary, even in childhood, but the dehumanization had ripped this part from me. And then my doctoral dissertation helped to heal me. It was literally writing my way through my identity that enabled me to unify the language and the feelings I had been having since I was very young. It all made sense to me. I began to think critically about how to take this knowledge, and what I had theorized in my dissertation, to create change not just for me but for the non-binary community. I wanted to make it possible for others to be seen as non-binary people, to assert our existence; I wanted to make this contribution to visibility. I needed to put it plainly into words that we exist — write about it, speak about it, and stamp it with my self.

I started to enact my non-binary visibility through my online writing and by posting images of myself, selfies mostly, on social media in 2016. My dissertation would exist forever, outlining my thoughts and ideas, set in that specific time and place, which already, in some places, feel outdated.

Yet I wanted my ideas to have a life outside of academia, where I could reach people. My first piece of published writing appeared in *HuffPost* on October 11, 2016, shortly after I'd completed my Ph.D. It was entitled "We Are Non-Binary Trans People and Yes, We Exist." I wrote about the lack of non-binary visibility and how our erasure from discourse contributes to transphobic perspectives about our existence, pointing to emerging legal recognition of our community and subsequent backlash. The article was read by tens of thousands of people within days of it going live. Seeing my face on the front page of *HuffPost* felt surreal, but it felt right. I was proud of making this contribution to non-binary visibility, and the responses to this article were incredibly supportive and appreciative. It was a turning point to transform my education into action. I discovered that I could make an intervention into the very problems I had examined in my doctoral research by writing short essays to confront non-binary erasure; I was turning my academic voice into practice.

The reach of these online outlets opened a space for me to inspire acceptance and to raise awareness for non-binary people. Around the time my first *HuffPost* piece was published, non-binary activists in the United States started to make headlines with their historic legal wins for non-binary recognition. Sara Kelly Keenan became one of the first people in the United States, and the first person in the state of California, to be legally recognized as non-binary. Keenan would then become the first American to be legally recognized as intersex on her birth certificate. These high-profile legal victories for non-binary recognition started to make the impossible feel possible. It was an articulation of our identity, under legal terms, on a public scale, that propelled the conversation forward and widened our visibility. It was then, in early 2017, that I began to think about how I too could be officially and legally recognized as a non-binary trans person in Canada.

A wave of non-binary legal recognition across North America followed Keenan's victories. In Canada, Gemma M. Hickey, a non-binary person living in Newfoundland and Labrador, became the first person to apply publicly for a non-binary birth certificate in their province and in the country as a whole. Seeing other non-binary people advocate for their legal recognition was the final piece of my own puzzle in reclaiming my identity. It was time to apply everything from my education and my past advocacy to contribute to this movement. I decided I had to act for myself.

When I decided to apply for my non-binary birth certificate in Ontario, it felt as though I was summoning a
new wave of strength and courage, but the truth is that
I had been preparing myself for this fight for a long time.
The application process itself was slow going. It took weeks
to gather the many documents and materials necessary
to challenge the absence of a non-binary birth certificate
option. I paid careful attention to every detail to avoid
making the kind of mistake the government could use to
reject my application out of hand. I reviewed the paper-
work meticulously, and I brought in experts to help me pull
together the evidence required to attest to my change of
sex designation from male to non-binary. The hardest part,
for me at least, was having to ask my doctor to confirm my
gender identity in an official letter—as if gender isn't self-
determined. Fortunately, she was amenable to confirming
my change of sex designation and wrote me the letter—her
first. The time it took to collect the various documents
and double-check the details felt like a necessary part of
the process; these were critical steps that were part of the
challenge. My hope was that the government would see
my attention to detail as a sign of the authenticity of my
determination to effect change.

During this time, I was living in Vancouver with Florian.
It was easy enough to assemble and submit my application from a distance, but I decided that wasn't going to be
enough. I wanted to bring attention to the issue, since I
knew that my application would challenge the system. This
would be a significant moment, not only for me but for all
non-binary people. So I decided to travel to Toronto to apply

in person at the central Service Ontario office. I also decided to go public with my application, involving the media and posting about my story on social media. I gave the exclusive story to CBC News in Toronto the day before I submitted my application. For me, that was the point of no return for my privacy, yet it was a powerful return to myself.

I applied for my non-binary Ontario birth certificate on May 12, 2017, making the explicit request for a non-binary designation by drawing a box on the application form and writing "male to non-binary" next to it. I won't lie, it was terrifying to make the personal so public. Yet I felt a force, a power within me, and it was impossible to ignore. Walking into the Service Ontario office in person, and seeing my intention through, called on the entirety of my life's experience. My voice carried with it every moment in my life when I spoke out against inequality, oppression, and abuse. I acted with everything in my mind, heart, and soul when I submitted my application. And I could feel past generations of trans warriors lifting me up through the process.

IN MAY 2017, as my fight for non-binary legal recognition in Canada began, I began to record my thoughts and feelings in a journal. We also started filming the process in the summer of 2017 to serve as footage for a documentary. Starting on the plane from Vancouver to Toronto, I wrote in an unfiltered way about my experiences over the next twelve months. I've included excerpts from some of these entries below.

May 11, 2017

I know there will be hate. There is always hate. People get scared when they don't understand, and they redirect this fear onto the easiest target: me.

I spent the day giving interviews. I imagine people driving in their cars, sitting at home, working in an office or a mechanics shop, listening to me speak about non-binary recognition, and hopefully ending their day with just a little more understanding and tolerance. I imagine parents going home and sitting down with their kids to discuss these ideas. I imagine families coming together around my words — perhaps even turning this tolerance into compassion for their children, their siblings, and their parents who are neither men nor women.

Tomorrow is the day.

May 12, 2017

I did it. I applied for my non-binary birth certificate while juggling several CBC News segments in Toronto. I am too tired to write anything else now. I gave everything today. I want to make our society a better place for non-binary people. I don't want them to have to cope with the incredible amount of stress, anxiety, and depression that results from being invisible.

May 13, 2017

I am on a train travelling through Napanee to Kingston. I wonder if I'll look up through the window at the right time to see a view of my old family home. I used to watch the train from our back porch.

I thought of something important today: The birth certificate issued to my parents shortly after my birth on July 10, 1982, was false. I have had to live with this lie for thirty-four years, and will have to put up with it for even longer if the Ontario government refuses to approve my application. I wonder how much this lie has contributed to my experiences with depression over my lifetime. Someone could argue that a birth certificate is merely a piece of paper and shouldn't have such an effect on me, but that person is probably already accepted, recognized, and included in society. The thing is, I'm not.

The birth certificate that I applied for yesterday is the truthful one — the one that I chose for myself, not what has been forced upon me by a system that fails to recognize my truth.

May 29, 2017

The anti-transphobia rally on Parliament Hill was symbolic for me. To turn a week of advocating for non-binary people in the public eye into action, standing on the hill in front of the media and over a hundred trans people and allies, was a moment that showed how my actions had come full circle. But I was paranoid almost the entire time. My story and my face had been everywhere. Standing there on the hill with MPP Cheri DiNovo, who has championed our community, I was worried that someone was going to ridicule me, assault me, harass me, erase me. I was thinking about protection, privacy, and shelter in those moments. How would I escape an attack? How would I deal with a verbal onslaught? This is how non-binary people often think in public, often when we have already put ourselves out there for scrutiny.

We flew home in the evening after the rally. The first morning back in Vancouver made me realize that I wouldn't be able to take a break from the press just yet. Cheri DiNovo questioned the Ontario Legislature, specifically the Minister in charge of birth certificates and Service Ontario, about my non-binary birth certificate application. The Minister's official response indicated that the government was following my story and that they would conduct consultations this summer and begin issuing gender-neutral birth certificates in 2018. This wasn't good enough for me because, under Ontario law, I have a right to receive my non-binary birth certificate in the same amount of time as every other Ontarian, within six weeks of the submission of my application.

I feel an enormous amount of pressure emanating from an axis of forces: governmental, societal, media-based, and even from my own family. Why wasn't this announcement good enough? Should I just accept this as a positive response to my application and allow the government to take the time they need to implement their new policy? No, because all these forces focused on the headline instead of the deeper issue — that it is beyond time non-binary people are socially and legally recognized in Ontario.

The attention that ensued from the national and international news elevated me to the status of a trans activist in Canada. I didn't ask for that title, and in some ways I'm a little uncomfortable with it, as I never wanted to become a spokesperson for the community in the eyes of the media. But my initial goal to reclaim my identity through proper legal recognition had evolved into a responsibility to enact change for members of my community. I wanted to contribute to legal recognition for non-binary people, not necessarily to be seen as a leader. In any event, there was no turning back now. I had embarked on a path to disrupt the status quo that recognized only "M" or "F" for sex and gender in Canada — and beyond. It still overwhelms me to think about the responsibility that came into my life from that day forward. People all over the country, and all over the world, began to contact me to share their stories and their gratitude for my advocacy. Their feelings of erasure fuelled my determination to keep moving forward. And their supportive and appreciative messages kept me optimistic and hopeful.

I had been motivated to apply for my non-binary birth certificate out of my own personal feelings of invisibility and erasure; I wanted to make myself visible in the eyes of the law. But after I went public, the non-binary community was constantly on my mind — non-binary children, their families, and non-binary adults who experienced the effects of erasure over and over again. I saw their faces in front of

me in their social media profiles and sometimes in person. I
knew I had to take this responsibility seriously. I'm not perfect, and I probably haven't met the expectations of every
single non-binary person and never will, but I know that I
have made a difference for many people.

I want to be totally clear: I am just one of *many* non-
binary people who have contributed to the realization of
non-binary legal recognition. To illustrate this point, I've
included a timeline at the end of this book (see page 249) to
highlight some of the monumental steps taken by our community during the period from June 2016 to October 2018. I
recommend you give it a read. It's really quite impressive!

The extensive legislation that was passed in the United
States and Canada from 2016 to 2018 is remarkable — revolutionary, even. However, neither country yet has comprehensive, nation-wide, legal recognition in place for all
of its non-binary citizens. Elsewhere in the world — in
Australia, Germany, India, Nepal, New Zealand, Pakistan,
the Netherlands, Austria, and Taiwan — laws have been
implemented to recognize *all* non-binary citizens, whether
in the form of the "X" designation (the acceptable and
widely used short form, often called gender-neutral, for
gender and sex that is neither M or F) on official government documents, full non-binary designation, or a specific
cultural recognition, similar to that which *hijra* people in
India have received.

· · ·

WHILE WAITING FOR the official response from the Government of Ontario in the summer of 2017, I received a letter from the province's Deputy Registrar General. I opened it on the edge of nerves. And then my heart sank, and I felt a wave of sickness. The letter outlined that the government had decided to deny, or possibly delay, my change of gender designation from male to non-binary. It was difficult to determine what exactly they were saying because little detail about their plans for a new policy were provided.

I found out that my application was marked as delayed. Ontario had placed my application on "pending" status while they conducted consultations and a policy review to "get it right." Adding a non-binary option on Ontario birth certificates wouldn't impact the majority of Ontario residents, so what did "get it right" really mean? The designation should be available to non-binary Ontarians who need their gender marker to match their true gender identity, so the government's excuse at the time troubled and further distressed me. A debate ensued about non-binary birth certificates in the province.

The Angus Reid Institute was tasked with conducting a survey of Ontarians to determine public opinion on the issue, and it cited my application as part of what was informing the sudden and vital discussion about non-binary birth certificates. While this was happening, I retained a team of Ontario-based lawyers—Michelle Thomarat of Dewart Gleason, and Mika Imai of Symes Street & Millard—to challenge the delay. Since Toby's Law was introduced in 2012 by my champion Cheri DiNovo, the Ontario Human Rights Code had explicitly protected gender identity, gender expression, and sex as prohibited grounds for discrimination, and since my application was denied on the basis of sex, gender identity, and gender expression, it was in conflict with the very law in place.

Then, in August 2017, Canada's federal government announced that it would finally start to recognize non-binary people with "X" designations on Canadian passports. Canada was catching up to the rest of the world. While this policy was being implemented, the federal government planned to provide an interim solution in the form of a temporary observation indicating that the sex marker "M" or "F" on the front page of the passport should be read as "X" or "unspecified." It was a landmark moment for non-binary visibility in Canada.

I visited the central passport office in Vancouver on the first day that the "X" gender observation became available to Canadians. The Passport Canada employees at that office explained that I was the first person in their Vancouver office to apply for the new observation. While that was exciting, I soon discovered that they were telling me this to excuse their need to involve managers to make sure they were processing my application correctly. I felt paranoid the entire time I was in that passport office. I thought that somehow I would be rejected, even though the new policy was officially in place.

That same month, since I resided in Vancouver, I felt that taking action in British Columbia was the next step: I wanted the short-form non-binary designation "X" on my combined health card and driver's licence. The "M" marker on my ID had been haunting me for too long. It was the

obvious next step to achieving full recognition as a non-
binary person on all my forms of identification, while waiting for Ontario's delay to play out. The New Democratic
Party (NDP) had recently formed a minority government in
British Columbia. As the NDP are known for their progres-
sive social democratic politics, I assumed that the government would react swiftly and favourably to my application.
The ruling party's response to my application—which was
a failure to respond—ignited another fight for legal recognition in a second province.

As a goodwill gesture, I sent a letter to prominent members of the NDP minority government months before publicly applying for my "X" designation. The only response
I received was from one minister who told me that a con-
sultation on the issue was underway and to let them know
if I wanted to be kept up to date. The government's lack
of response to my letter was heartbreaking since I had
always supported and worked with the NDP, both feder-
ally and provincially, in my advocacy. I had even met Jack
Layton while he was the leader of the party. So I repeated
my Ontario plan in British Columbia. I publicly applied for
my "X" designation in August 2017. I had to wait twenty
business days for an official response from the B.C. government after submitting the application.

In the meantime, I took legal action with my team in
Ontario by filing a complaint with the Human Rights
Tribunal four months after my non-binary birth certificate application had been delayed. In an overwhelming
convergence, my Ontario and B.C. legal fights both escalated on the same day. On September 28, 2017, the day that I

submitted the human rights complaint in Ontario, the B.C. government outright rejected my application for correct non-binary markers on my provincially issued identification, which I found out only by contacting them directly to query the status of my application.

September 28, 2017

Last night was full of worry. I had planned to be interviewed about the filing of my human rights application in the Human Rights Tribunal of Ontario for my non-binary birth certificate. What I didn't know was that I would also have to re focus on my application for my "X" gender markers in British Columbia. I didn't know that a simple phone call to inquire about the status of my application twenty-one days after it was registered would be met with such a ferocious and unkind denial of my application and my right to receive my "X" markers on these forms of identification. When I called the Health Insurance system, the first person I spoke with told me that my application had "missing information." This representative was perplexed because typically they send out letters to applicants to inform them about the "missing information," but no such letter had been sent out to me. My call was escalated to an enrolment specialist who seemed emboldened by what she read in front of her on the computer screen. She firmly noted that "X" is simply not possible on B.C. identifications and that there are only two options available to me: male and female.

I woke up yesterday facing what has oddly become a familiar experience in my life lately—dealing with the media's questions on something very personal, my gender identity and my decision to take legal action against a government entity. It is necessary to go public because non-binary people are so invisible and erased. My voice is my weapon to carve down the crumbling edifice that the government perpetuates by only counting people as male or female—nothing else. I could feel my emotions swelling—sadness, frustration, even anger overcame me. It is a dangerous moment when a government entity enacts gender-based discrimination. When this happens, some members of society can feel warranted to discriminate against non-binary people. As a non-binary trans person, I will continue to fight. My conviction is strong, but I need our governments to stand up, to join us in this fight, and to protect all of us.

The rejection of my application in British Columbia left me feeling a deep distress. I decided to file a human rights application in the province, with lawyer Frances Mahon, to challenge the denial of my correct non-binary gender markers. It is easy to get lost in the process of the battle for legal change. The process consumes energy and attention, especially when the very thing I was fighting for seemed as though it was becoming more difficult and complex to achieve, with multiple legal challenges and advocacy efforts underway. I was trying to do my part in Canada to arrive at a place in society where people who are neither men nor women could be legally recognized and respected.

For months, I waited for the governments to act; it felt like years. My human rights complaints argued that the government had breached my human rights on the grounds of sex, gender identity, and gender expression. But what was I supposed to do while I waited to be recognized? I've never been the most patient person, but I had to surrender to the process. Didn't Ontario and British Columbia realize that each day with incorrect gender markers on my IDs not only exposed me to continued distress and anxiety but also contributed to the distress and anxiety of numerous other non-binary people?

I felt vulnerable and helpless while waiting for the laws to catch up with reality with respect to human rights in this country. Of course, I can't equate the struggle of non-binary people to achieve social recognition with our correct gender markers with other human rights violations that are committed in many parts of the world. For example, our fight for recognition is not the same as combatting the illegality of same-sex sexuality, which often results in physical violence and sometimes murder.

The despair that I faced while waiting prompted me to continue taking action, to continue applying pressure. I wrote new op-ed pieces in VICE News and *HuffPost*, discussing the benefits of officially recognizing non-binary people with correct gender markers. And then I decided to travel to Toronto to show the politicians that I meant business, that I would not be ignored. My responsibility to my community necessitated that non-binary gender markers be made available to all non-binary residents. I had to keep acting for non-binary youth, adults, and parents who didn't have a voice. I had to show the government what my determination looks like in person. My thinking was that they couldn't ignore me if I was standing in front of them, face to face.

I travelled to Toronto in November 2017 to visit the Ontario Legislature. I was prepared to meet the lawmakers in person, including the premier of the province, Kathleen Wynne, if it came to that. I wanted them to feel the heart of my advocacy. I wanted them to know the humanity of the issue. This wasn't just about me; this was about our society. It was about allowing those of us who feel stifled by the binary to be a little more free with our identity, and to feel protected by a government that recognizes who we are. I wanted them to feel the distress I was experiencing on a daily basis by constantly having to present ID that didn't match the reality of my identity.

My visit to the Ontario Legislature was at the official invitation of my political champion, MPP Cheri DiNovo. Cheri is unwavering in her commitment to the trans community. I could tell from our very first meeting that she would champion my cause. She understood the urgency of our need to be legally recognized after being invisible and erased for so long. Cheri is a brave and brilliant woman. There is remarkable action behind her pressing political words. And her path is guided by her heart. She's passed more LGTBQ bills than any other politician in Canadian history. She gets things done! The world would be a much better place if there were more politicians like Cheri DiNovo.

This was my first time at the Ontario Legislature. My steadfast lawyer, Mika Imai, joined me for the visit on November 27, 2017. It was a very cold day in Toronto, yet the bright sun gave me a sense of hope. I arrived at Queen's Park a short distance from the front entrance of the Legislature and captured a short video for my social media pages. Florian was capturing B-roll for our documentary, and I was preparing myself for what was to come. How would I face them with the truth? Was I even ready for this? Would I come across more truthfully if I just let myself feel all of the wild emotions running through me that morning—the exhaustion, the worry, the stress? No, I had to be both myself and something else to appeal to all of them; I had to embody strength and perseverance, face them with composure, but also let myself be seen as an honest human being who is obviously distressed, which was the picture of truth.

Walking into the assembly and being faced with a full view of the governing party, the Ontario Liberal Party, forced me to sit with a whole host of uncomfortable emotions. In some part, I felt naked, exposed and open, while I sat there. The politicians started to pile into their seats, their demeanour blending a posturing facade with a truthful promise for their various political purposes. It took almost the entire hour of Question Period to reach Cheri's question about the delay of my non-binary birth certificate application and the resulting human rights complaint. With a respectful ferocity, Cheri directed the question to the Honourable Minister Tracey MacCharles, who was the Minister of Government and Consumer Services (the ministry in charge of Service Ontario), in the absence of the premier. Then, in an assertive tone, she asked the members of the government to look directly at me in the public gallery. I imagine they started to see the face of the issue at that point.

I took hold of Florian's hand and I started to cry. I couldn't hold back my emotions. The pressure that I was feeling from the dozens of politicians looking at me was impossible to ignore, so I was just going to feel it. I gave in to vulnerability. I was supported by Florian, my lawyers, Cheri, and other sympathetic MPPs, but I felt pinned to the wall by the pressure of their gaze. I'm only human. I don't represent the entirety of the issue. I was one person sitting there in front of them with tears streaming down my face. So much for composure.

After Question Period, Cheri arranged a brief meeting between me and the Honourable Minister MacCharles. What was I going to say? Could I even meet her face to face while I was so angry and upset by the delay? MacCharles joined us outside the doors to the legislative assembly. We shook hands, and I forgot about everything that I had planned to say when our eyes met. I just spoke from my heart. I could feel her heart. She was kind, and it was obvious that she empathized with me in some way. We looked into each other's eyes, into each other's souls. I felt as though she accepted my story. I could sense that she understood the humanity behind my face, the issue in front of her. My vital purpose for being there in person was to humanize my story, to help humanize our community, and I felt as though it had worked. At the very least, she got to see me beyond the news headlines. I left that meeting uncertain about the future, yet aware that something had shifted

At the end of 2017, both the Ontario and the British Columbia Human Rights Tribunals accepted my complaints. This acceptance appealed to the respective provinces to either agree to settlement discussions or prove legal rationale for the alleged discrimination that I had faced as a result of the delays and denials. We engaged in confidential discussions with both provinces in early 2018. Months later, I was able to share positive news with the public.

April 19, 2018

I'm an amazon, a fucking warrior. I have survived so much. I can get through this, and I will. It's so easy to focus on the worry and fear instead of the victory. I feel like I am moving closer to the end — a feeling that seemed unattainable last week.

I am trying to hold on to the victory, the hope it will create, the lives it might save, the hearts it will warm. I'm at the intersection of many different paths in my life right now. Seeing beyond what's right in front of me is a survival mechanism. It is also obscuring the moments of my life where I am making magic, weaving and casting spells from within my reservoir of purpose and passion. I am doing it. I am contributing to change, the great tidal shift in our culture. I am doing this. I just have to remind myself in the moment to enjoy it, to revel in the victory instead of always preparing for what's to come, the next battle, the new fight since it always seems like I am having to fight for respect and dignity.

People ask why I have to fight, why can't I just accept my position in society and live my life? Well, it's for that very reason that I have to fight. It gets exhausting to explain myself over and over again, to reassert myself, and to try to get people to understand me. At the very least, I deserve to be respected and valued as a human being. Yet, I don't always receive this dignity from other people. I find myself getting stretched thin by the inability of people to see me like any other human being. It's always Joshua the game-changer, Joshua the ground-breaker, Joshua the transgender person, Joshua the shit-disturber who never shuts up. Intimidating as I might be to some people, I am just hoping for validation and respect like every other human being. It's tough to always be treated like the one who sticks out from the crowd, the black sheep, and yes, I suppose that I am putting myself out there to be visible and vocal, but the purpose is beyond just me. This is bigger than Joshua. It is more than me. I am fighting for the hundreds of thousands of trans people across Canada and the millions beyond who have to face suffering, stigma, and fear because of who we are. This is why I will never give up.

May 4, 2018

I typed "Service Ontario birth certificate" into Google after returning to Canada from a trip overseas. Clicking on the link, I scrolled down to the part of

the website listing change of sex designation information. There it is. The policy in all its glory sitting there
completely public on the Service Ontario website. The
policy clearly states that a person with an Ontario
birth certificate can apply for a change of sex designation to Male (M), Female (F), and Non-Binary (X).
It also included a sentence with the other part of the
two-fold policy, the so-called gender-neutral option
which now provides an option to apply to have sex
designation removed from birth certificates entirely.
I could hardly believe my eyes. It's finally real.

I want people to know. They have a right to know.
This is a victorious day not just for me, but for the
entire community, for all of humanity.

I now have my birth certificate in hand. Well,
maybe not literally in hand, but it's with my Dad in
Ottawa. The documents are sitting safely in my old
bedroom, where I sat in my early twenties gazing out
at the stars, wishing for love that was granted with
Florian, and wishing to change lives, to save lives, to
make life just a bit easier for myself and others. My
wish has been granted. It's a wonderful feeling to be
officially recognized and counted by the place of my
birth for who I really am. Ironically, the X-Men were
one of my favourite super-hero teams growing up,
and the treatment of their mutations bears a striking
analogy to the experience of LGBTQ people. And now,
I am literally an "X-(Man)/(male)" — it actually says it
on the registration of my birth. "Male" is now in par-
enthesis with an "X" outside of the brackets beside it.

Joshua the X-male. The truth of this is actually quite funny, and it makes me feel good.

I am counting down the moments to when I can finally hold my new birth certificate in my hands. I will run in that door, up the stairs and into my room, rip open the envelope, and hold it close to my heart.

On May 7, 2018, I went public with the news that I had become the first person in Ontario to be issued a non-binary birth certificate. I had to prepare myself for this day, and it didn't come easy. I wrote about my experience in an op-ed piece for the *Toronto Star*.

MY NON-BINARY BIRTH CERTIFICATE
A VICTORY FOR THE TRANS COMMUNITY

Almost one year ago, on May 12, 2017, I walked into the central Service Ontario office in Toronto to apply for my non-binary birth certificate. I had no idea about the challenges and the emotional roller-coaster that faced me.

After Ontario delayed my application, and a subsequent human rights application, finally, I now have my non-binary birth certificate. It's a victory for me. It's a victory for our community.

After years of having the system define me, that has now changed. With the new Service Ontario policy for birth certificates, people in the province now have a choice beyond male and female on their birth certificates and it illustrates that non-binary people exist — we are Ontarians and we are Canadians.

The province has made history by becoming the first jurisdiction in the world to implement a twofold policy for birth certificates.

Birth certificates are now more inclusive. The policy achieves a respectful balance by recognizing non-binary people who want official sex markers, trans and cis people who don't want any sex markers at all, and the men, women and children who do not want these policy changes to affect their birth certificates.

To be clear, on the birth certificates of newborn children, parents will still be able to designate M, F or now an X (especially for the 1 in 1,500 babies born intersex), or they can choose not to list the sex designation of their child at all—allowing their child to one day self-determine their gender identity. The policy will have zero impact on the majority of Ontarians who want their birth certificates to stay the same.

Every time a trans person is forced to present a piece of ID designating incorrect sex markers, it exposes us to anxiety and distress because it is a vital part of our existence in society.

Commonplace experiences, such as travelling through airports, attending school and picking up parcels, can turn into stressful and painful events for trans people when we are forced to present personal information that does not match who we are.

Frequently, when I present my ID with an M or Male listed, the postal worker, bank teller, airport employee looks at me like there is something wrong with me because my ID doesn't match what I look like. These situations can range from stares to questioning the validity of my ID and therefore my existence.

Ontario's new policy will save lives.

It will have a profound positive impact on the lives of trans people. It will give people a choice for their birth certificates and it will give hope to trans people across the country who still live in provinces with governments that fail to recognize who they are, especially people who are neither men nor women.

In part, motivating a policy that officially recognizes non-binary people in Ontario has become one of my proudest moments. I was tormented as a gender-nonconforming child, teenager and young adult at the hands of people who verbally harassed and physically assaulted me. I don't want other children to grow up feeling the sting of another person's fist or the sharp, dehumanizing verbal abuse because their gender identity or expression isn't officially recognized and protected on government-issued ID.

Research from the University of Texas emphasizes that trans youth have suicidal thoughts at twice the rate of their peers, and 1 out of 3 trans youth have considered suicide.

The National Center for Transgender Equality in the U.S. states: "gender incongruent ID exposes people to a range of negative outcomes, from denial of employment, housing and public benefits to harassment and physical violence."

Trans Pulse at Western University "found a significant decrease in suicide risk among those who had ID documents matching their expressed gender. Having proper ID was found to have the potential to prevent 90 in 1,000 trans people from seriously considering suicide."

What matters is that people value and respect each other even if we don't agree. To elevate basic dignity for one another is the power of our shared humanity.

It was one of the most intense moments of my life. So much had led up to it. I was overwhelmed with it all. Everything came full circle — an entire year of fighting, worrying, and stressing out about all the possible outcomes — and finally I had claimed my victory.

On the morning of May 7, as the media was picking up on the story, Florian and I made our way to meet Kathleen Monk, an expert in communications who kindly supported me, at the Human Rights Monument in Ottawa for a press conference. I was feeling my nerves, but I was prepared. I stood confident in front of the monument, where many human rights activists had stood before me, knowing that this policy would save lives. The day was about my fight, and my victory — but it was also more than that. The weight of responsibility loosened its grip on me and I felt free.

I posted a one-minute video taken with my iPhone to Twitter on May 8; it showed me discussing the news and its significance for the non-binary community in Canada and beyond. Twitter made it a "Twitter Moment," and I was surprised to see that the video received over fifty-thousand views within just a few hours. The story of my victory was featured in the national press; NowThis News created a video about the story that generated more than three hundred thousand views; and then NBC News reported on it, which brought an international audience into the mix. It was scary, but I knew how important the moment was for non-binary visibility. I could hear my champions cheering me on.

FIGHTING FOR LEGAL RECOGNITION opened new creative opportunities for me. Earlier, I had helped foster non-binary representation and awareness with our film *Limina*, and now I felt as though I had to do more. I felt like it was time to tell my story, to bear my truth visually in artistic form. I wanted to carve out the space of non-binary representation to create representation where it doesn't exist.

Two chapters in my doctoral dissertation analyzed trans representation in documentary film. I had studied many trans documentaries in detail. The way that some of these films captured their subjects, manipulated their stories, sensationalized their lives, and objectified bodies was a pattern of representation that I wanted to move beyond. Many trans documentaries focus on similar narratives of trans identity: representing a trans person's transition. I saw the same transition story over and over again, just with different people. But I didn't see my transition story in these films. I wanted my kind of trans representation to be included in the landscape of documentary cinema. So I embarked on a path to create my own representation.

The idea for a documentary about my life first came up while I was fighting for legal recognition. Early in the fight, after I had publicly applied for my Ontario non-binary birth certificate in May 2017, I was approached by a number of Canadian funding bodies and networks with interest in creating a film about my advocacy. I knew from the beginning that if we were to tell my story in a documentary it would have to be intimate, personal, and highly subjective. I didn't want the influence of a major broadcaster altering my story to fit business objectives. I opened up to those around me I trusted most, asking for their advice. Wisdom came from a good friend of mine, Jules Arita Koostachin, who advised me from her own experience with storytelling and truth-telling.

Jules, who was born in Moose Factory, Ontario, is Cree from Moshkekowok territory, a member of Attawapiskat First Nation. With a rich background in documentary film-making, Jules is a matriarch who values truth above all else, and her approach to interviewing respects her subjects to the extent that I feel there is nothing object-related in her mind. Her films are often created from the seat of her ancestry, her family, and the subjects she loves. She tells stories because she has to. Jules sees who I am. Her gaze cuts through the colonial mentality. She sees me with many genders, beautiful and free. It is a relief to be around her, and to have her in my life. Her love for storytelling drew her to discuss my own life and what it might look like in documentary form.

Florian and I engaged in a discussion with Jules about what a documentary could focus on. Jules and Florian would combine their experience by co-directing and I would be the sole producer, to be in control of my own story. Together, we wrote a rough outline for a short documentary with a story arc taking the audience on a path from my childhood to adulthood, when I reclaimed myself and my identity. The film, appropriately titled *Non-Binary*, turned to crowdfunding. We received a very encouraging response. With our budget in hand, we shot the film in natural settings in and around Vancouver, used B-roll from our multiple trips to Ontario, and combed through archival video and images from my life. We were able to access a panoply of family footage shot by my Pop Stuart, my Poppa Joe (my mom's father), and my dad. In the end, *They Are Joshua* evolved from a short to a feature-length documentary due to a significant amount of material for the story and my evolving fight for recognition.

They Are Joshua portrays a different kind of transition story. I didn't know this until we saw a rough cut of the film. Instead of showing medical transitions or tragic stories, this trans documentary is a victory story. Yes, there is trauma, but my transition is about reconnecting with the child that got lost along the way in the myth that gender is only man and woman. The documentary excavates moments from my life that seemed impossible to ever revisit, to ever portray. There is something powerful that the visual medium can achieve that the written word is unable to uncover. It unearths what language cannot, and what I haven't been able to articulate. When I watched the cut of the film in a theatre space during post-production, I couldn't stop crying. I was completely overwhelmed by the complementary yet contrasting images of me as a child and now as an adult, fully confident with my identity in the present day. I found myself made real and material in a powerful way by receiving my non-binary birth certificate.

They Are Joshua illuminates this reconnection, and that's why it's such an important story to share.

TWELVE

The Amazon

I'LL CALL HER Mrs. Thornton — her real name is disguised in these pages to protect her privacy and that of her family, a name carrying the weight of darkness that still stirs within me. Mrs. Thornton found her power in oppressing the most vulnerable and marginalized, and I'm sure she was surprised that she met her match with me, a little six-year-old kid.

I was in grade one at elementary school in 1988. That year, we lived in Chapleau, a remote town in Northern Ontario with fewer than one thousand inhabitants. The town is isolated, surrounded by wilderness. My memories from up north are mostly happy ones. Laura, one of my best friends, lived a short walk from my home, and our days were filled with playing some of the earliest available computer games and exploring the woods. Robert was another good friend, and we also played games and explored the outdoors together. I cared deeply for both of them. I still do. The happiness on my face in family videos from that time is undeniable. But I also see a warrior at that age, eyes wide open, preparing for what was to come.

Mrs. Thornton was a severe and strict teacher. She embodied the climate of the town, cold and hard. Her life force seemed as though it had been drained by the decades of isolation that I presume she'd already lived through there. But instead of strengthening herself as a survivor, willing to help ease the suffering of others by extending her compassion, she succumbed to weakness and instead took her pain out on children.

Mrs. Thornton physically and psychologically abused some of my classmates. She never touched me, but I watched as she snapped rulers against my friends' fingers, or slapped their faces, or aggressively grabbed their bodies to position them "properly" in their chairs. I witnessed her assaulting my classmates multiple times. I was a child; they were children. It took time for me to process how wrong her actions were, but I knew something wasn't right.

This was the first time I had ever witnessed physical and emotional abuse. I sat powerless in my seat, with a sick feeling in my stomach, watching her mistreat other kids.

It was confusing at first. I was scared to act. But then one day I'd had enough. I didn't like the sick feeling I always had at school. I couldn't stand the crying and sad faces of the other kids. Clarity rushed through me like a wave and made me take a stand. I had to say something, and I had to do something. I asked Mrs. Thornton to excuse me from class to visit the bathroom, and then I knew what I had to do. I walked right past the bathroom, down the stairs, and into the principal's office. I had never gone to his office before, but I had a purpose, and a power was propelling me to act. I said to him, directly, "Mrs. Thornton is hitting my friends in class!"

The principal called my parents into an urgent meeting. The school's administration responded swiftly, and Mrs. Thornton was formally disciplined. My parents were obviously disturbed by what was happening in my classroom, but I could also sense the pride that was pounding loudly in their hearts because I had stood up for my classmates.

One day, shortly after Mrs. Thornton's abuse had been exposed, she visited me at home. The school had insisted that she atone for her violence by visiting the homes of all the kids who were affected, homes where children had brought their painful confusion back home with them after witnessing, or being of the victim of, her violent behaviour. I stood in between my parents, secure in their presence. And after she apologized, I looked up at her and I said, "Please don't do that again." I don't remember those words myself, but my plea to her remains crystal clear in my parents' minds. It was a significant point in my childhood, when my parents realized the depth of my strength, the potential for me to be a leader, an advocate, even a warrior.

This was the beginning of my story as an Amazon. Or what I like to call myself: Trans Amazon. I feel sad now for my child and young adult self, realizing the extent of the dehumanization, bullying, harassment, and assaults. Looking at childhood images of my happy, smiling face, I want to reach out to let myself know that I will survive the coming onslaught. I want to be kind to the history of who I am and where I came from. I want to say to my six-year-old self: "It will be tough trying, even like a waking nightmare at times, but you know that you are strong. You are loved, and you will be loved. You are a warrior. People will be hurtful, they will be violent, but they will empower you and make you resilient. You will find the way to help other people because of your resilience. Your fight for survival, and the fight for others, will both soften and harden your body, heart, and spirit, but you were born to be the Amazon."

I can imagine myself in Themyscira, the fictional island nation of the Amazons imagined by DC Comics for the *Wonder Woman* franchise. But my version of Themyscira is slightly different. My island would be populated by women, non-binary people, and gender-nonconforming people who would be able to find refuge there from misogyny and trans misogyny. The island would serve as a place for both retreat and preparation to resist the forces of patriarchy that gain power by maintaining the status quo of the gender binary.

It's my fantasy. My reimagined idea of being an Amazon manifested when, to survive, I had to surround myself with strong women to stand by my side. Without the support of women (cis and trans), non-binary people, and gender-nonconforming people, I'm not sure I would have made it to live beyond the dehumanization that I've faced.

The Amazons of myth, famous archers, were said to remove one of their breasts in order to improve the bow's position on their chest and perfect their aim in battle. When I first encountered this idea, although proved false by academia, I felt that this practice corresponded to the metamorphosis of my own body and the empowerment that I now feel. Of course, I haven't embarked on transitioning for the sake of physical battle. I can't deny that my transitioning, especially the way I've modified my body, has been about minimizing the amount of violence that I've faced in my life, that I could face, as a person who visually disturbs the gender binary.

In part, my transitioning has healed me, and it lessens my exposure to harassment. Before the facial hair removal, and the effect of hormones on my skin, voice, and body, my appearance was more explicitly disruptive of the binary. I don't enjoy the necessity of having to always be on, and ready to fight. I don't mean physically fight someone, necessarily; I'm thinking more of the spirited fight needed for self-protection, to be able to walk away, escape, and deflect harassment. It can be exhausting to embody a self-protection that is always switched on. Human beings shouldn't have to be constantly in self-defence mode. Gender-nonconforming people, especially those of us with expressions and identities that don't line up with what is expected of us, are forced to confront bigotry in dangerous forms. The fact that I, and members of my community, particularly trans and gender-nonconforming people of colour, have to be ready to protect ourselves if someone's fear or hate is triggered by our appearance or presence should be reason enough for our society to do everything in its power to eradicate transphobia. No child should be exposed to the violence that I have faced in my life, and that other trans, non-binary, and gender-nonconforming people face.

Think of that resonant image of the Amazons—dressed in trousers, perhaps with exposed breasts or even bound breasts, riding horses, carrying long spears or swords signifying a phallic power—these are characteristics that people of all genders can embody. I have all of these things: a hybrid body and a warrior spirit to fiercely protect my family, my friends, and, at times in my life, other marginalized people.

One of the first references in literature to the Amazons is in Homer's *Iliad*, where Amazons are referred to as *"amazones antianeirai."* The word *antianeirai* has contributed to a confusion around Amazons being "man-haters." Dr. Adrienne Mayor's *The Amazons*, although fixated on a binary understanding of gender in her book, suggests that the meaning of this word is closer to "equals of men," not "opposites of men," so *"amazones antianeirai"* translates to "amazons, the equals." These equals were considered "others"—sometimes gender ambiguous, sometimes monstrous —a plurality of people existing in various parts of the world at the time. Isn't that what we should strive for? Now it makes sense why they waged all of those battles. It seems they were fighting for something powerful: equality.

Another aspect of Themyscira, one that is often represented as being a part of Amazon culture, is the freeing quality of the wild natural environment, which complements the idea of existing outside of the constricting forces of the gender binary in society. The natural environment and plentiful wildlife of the tiny northern town of Chapleau nourished the strength of my spirit and my body and made me feel as though I was on my own island of sorts. Even in

Napanee we lived in the countryside near fields and creeks, and I found a power in being myself at home in untamed nature. The sound of wolves calling, black bears, moose, bird species too plentiful to count, and going fishing with my dad—it all made me fall in love with non-human sentient life. I fell in love with the wild and fluid.

That the power of nature is both wild and free has always made sense to me on a deep level. Even at a young age, I felt a familiarity with nature that would come to evolve and offer me serenity. I became emboldened by the resilience, the challenge of the living facing survival or death in the natural world. While so much of my life has felt like swimming against the tide, my connection to nature and to my warrior spirit has transformed me. I've always felt at home out there beyond the system of a culture that excluded me.

I am an Amazon now.

The dehumanization transformed my flesh and my heart into armour.

It called forth a strength of spirit that can be found in the unyielding life force, from the most microscopic of bacteria to the enormous power of old-growth trees.

The greatest influences in my life have been powerful women, cis and trans, and later non-binary and gender-nonconforming people. I am a mosaic of the people who have empowered me, stood by me, inspired me, and who *see* me.

A mosaic of Amazons in these pages. I am now one. Joshua, the Amazon.

THIRTEEN

The Philosopher

I found ME in my resilience.
I found MYSELF in my storytelling,
And I found THEY in other people's stories.

CRITICS OF NON-BINARY GENDER and sex would tell you that it is impossible for most people to imagine themselves outside of the dominant cultural scripts written for us at birth. Even some feminist gender theory argues that gender identity and gender itself are immutable. It's old news to think that gender is fixed or that we can't change our gender identity.

Gender is self-determined and isn't immutable. Some parts of Western culture are shifting towards an acknowledgement that there is a freedom in how we identify ourselves. In truth, gender diverse people have always been here, but the younger generations are showing us the way.

At the heart of my resilience are my stories. I found me within my story of survival, and I found myself through the act of telling my story; it was through the writing of this book that I was able to reconnect with myself, the person I was born to be. Non-binary, for me, is about abundance, freedom to grow and change, as I evolve. Yet I haven't painted the entire picture of how I found they/them — the discovery of the space in language where I exist, found in the stories of others, and of a return to nature that made finding myself possible again.

This is the final piece of my story, where I found *they*: the place in language and in society, and on the outside of culture, that I could define for *me* and *myself*. This final piece is not an ending; it is a new beginning — the start of my life when I can finally be who I am.

I CONSTANTLY SEEK VALIDATION from others. It's tough for me to share this with you. I feel weak admitting that I yearn for validation. Why seek validation if I'm already confident about who I am? The truth is that, sometimes, I feel an intense lack of confidence about my thoughts, my work, and my contributions to my community. I feel an emptiness where my self-confidence should reside. I should be certain of myself, but, to tell you the truth, I don't really know that much at all. And that's okay. I'm still struggling to be a better human being, to be respected, and, even better, to be accepted and appreciated for who I am. I am learning and yearning for validation just like you. We all want to be valid.

I seek this validation from Florian, my parents, my brothers, my close friends, and even acquaintances, to whom I turn for reassurance. Often, I think to myself, *I am doing a good job today, being a good and acceptable human today, if someone tells me that I am.* I realize that I don't need to be validated to know that I'm a human being, but it just feels better to know that people accept me. The dehumanization in my life makes me insecure. As someone who is open to being in flux, not feeling stable, secure, and static in a fixed identity, I often feel as though I am living without established parameters or safe boundaries. Being open and fluid has helped me find myself, but I do tend to get lost when my feelings of societal erasure are too intense. Receiving validation helps bring me back to myself.

I've endeavoured to lay out the layers of my life and my identity to lessen my invisibility, but also the invisibility of all non-binary people. To live in this invisible/visible space is a subjective experience that is founded in an internal and external conflict. Non-binary people must fight for our right to exist, and this does something to the soul. The conflict makes us resilient, but it also means that we must deal with an unusual amount of external interrogation when people fail to see us as fellow human beings.

The knowledge that non-binary people exist eluded me for most of my life, until a few stories and theories, shared in books, resonated with me. Stories beyond the binary were told in the margins of discussion about gender. Kate Bornstein changed my life with their first book, published in 1994, *Gender Outlaw: On Men, Women, and the Rest of Us.* Their perspective on gender identity, with statements like "I don't call myself a woman, and I know I'm not a man," felt honest, familiar, and it was groundbreaking. Could it really be possible for a person to be neither a man nor a woman, as Bornstein's title and stories suggested? Part memoir and part academic investigation, their book presented layers of evidence from their life to show that being beyond the binary was possible. It was a revolutionary act that made sense. I furiously wrote notes that filled up the margins of the book upon my first reading and went through it a second and third time to dive deeper into the familiarity that I felt with their story. It became clear to me that gender conformity is an iterative script constructed by the powerful in society to fool us into thinking that we can't thrive in our human variance. The "rest of us" existed, according to Bornstein. Their life proved it. Here it was — the missing link meant to stay invisible and hidden to those of us who feel outside of the system of gender.

I read the book in 2010, and I wanted more. Fortunately, Bornstein's story wasn't the only one that existed at the time. I found more proof to substantiate the feelings I was having about what I thought were the only two available identities: man or woman. I didn't feel like picking one. I didn't feel like either one, so why did I have to choose?

Leslie Feinberg's *Transgender Warriors: Making History from Joan of Arc to Dennis Rodman* contained another key to unlock the meaning of being a possible subject beyond the binary. The book showcased a wealth of historical and cultural examples of trans men, trans women, and gender-nonconforming people (who, if the language had existed then, might have been understood as having non-binary gender expression or identity). Bornstein and Feinberg helped me find the inclusive "they" language that contributed to making the articulation of our identity possible, even if these authors weren't using "they" at the time they both wrote their books. Jack Halberstam's *Female Masculinity* was another source of wonderful knowledge containing proof of gender diversity and illustrating the wide array of possible gender expressions then categorized as "female masculinity."

Non-binary people were mostly invisible to me before I found their stories shared in books. Many non-binary people still feel invisible to themselves. Anyone can feel invisible when it comes to parts of who you are; that doesn't have to be related to gender identity and expression. From the debates raging about gender dysphoria in childhood, and the gender-affirmative care of children, to trans women being recognized as women with the same rights and access to cis women's spaces and gender-neutral pronouns; to the blue-in-the-face insisting that "there are only two genders" bullshit, we are constantly being juggled and judged by people who act to delegitimize our right to exist and self-identify as we are. We are, in fact, hated by some simply for being who we are. And the cause of this hatred is bigotry because the rationale people use for delegitimizing members of our community just doesn't hold up to facts, lived experience, and yes, science.

We all have a right to express our opinions. This book is full of my opinions, housed within my personal stories. But don't we also deserve basic human dignity and respect?

I see through the lens of my perspective and my

experiences, fully situated in my stories, just as your opinions are viewed through your own lens. Being born in 1982, at roughly the beginning of the "Millennial" generation, has helped me to speak from the edge of this generational perspective while also being aware of how the next cohort, "Generation Z," is accelerating the conversation around non-binary gender identity and expression.

Trans people, non-binary people, and gender-nonconforming people are more common than most people think. In 2015, the National Center for Transgender Equality, an advocacy organization for trans people in the United States, published a significant report after surveying almost twenty-eight thousand members of the trans community across America. According to their study, a large component of the trans community (36 percent) identifies as non-binary. In 2017, GLAAD (the organization originally known as the Gay and Lesbian Alliance Against Defamation), published a study showing that as many as 12 percent of Millennials identify as trans or gender-nonconforming. Another study, from 2016, conducted by one of the leading trend forecasting agencies in the United States, J. Walter Thompson Innovation Group, emphasizes the generational shift that I've alluded to among the Millennial generation and Generation Z: the Thompson report showed that 56 percent of the people in Generation Z (known as "Gen Zers") knew someone who used they/them pronouns, compared to 43 percent of Millennials. Almost half of the Gen Z respondents and about a third of Millennials self-identified as a sexuality other than heterosexual. These respondents identified in the middle range (1–5) on a spectrum of

sexuality with heterosexual and homosexual at opposite
ends of a scale ranging from 0 to 6 (0 being completely
heterosexual and 6 completely homosexual).

If that's not enough to highlight the generational shift
with respect to gender and sexuality beyond the binary, the
University of California, Los Angeles, conducted a state-
wide survey from 2015 to 2016 which indicated that 27 percent of people between the ages of twelve and seventeen are
viewed as gender-nonconforming by their classmates. This
suggests that 27 percent of youth in California (or 796,000)
have a gender-nonconforming expression or are viewed to
have a gender-nonconforming expression.

The statistics show that non-binary identity and expression are actually more "normal" and "natural" than we
think. But what is "normal" and "natural" anyway? I've
been taught to stay away from using "normal" or "natural" to describe anything, but I want to turn these words
on their head to delve deeper. I want to think about these
words in a non-binary way. After all, these words are not
universally understood. We have such a simplistic picture
when it comes to sex and gender, and what's "normal" or
"natural" is fixed by culture. The boundaries of our humanity are much more complex than what is suggested by the
cultural binary of normal versus abnormal.

What is deemed socially acceptable and typically practised by the majority of people is considered normal by
most. Normal is subjective. We don't all agree on what is
normal. It's up for debate, open to opinion, and it changes
over time. How we understand the normal may change,
just as our concept of gender changes over time. Normal is

a commonality shared among many people that we expect all people to follow. But how we understand normal for human beings is changing. "Normal" marriage used to be straight marriage. Not any more. The "normal" nuclear family structure used to be a man, a woman, and children. Not any more. "Normal" voting rights in North America excluded Indigenous people, black people, and women for centuries. Not any more. What is normal changes, and it should change as society shifts and as we evolve as human beings. The normal is not set in stone.

"Natural," on the other hand, is a tricky word. Many would argue that the state of our bodies at birth is "natural." How we are determined by our essential biological traits is thought of as our most "natural" state. In fact, the transphobic argument that sex and gender are "immutable biological facts" has been used as political agency against our community.

The way we think about the natural stems from our understanding of nature, but we rarely think about nature beyond the simplistic notion of it that has been constructed for us by our culture. Culture aims to reduce the natural world to understandable terms — to know all there is to know. But nature is much more complex, wild, and free than this. In fact, it is in nature that we find aberrations of the natural, adaptations over time that challenge nature's supposed "fixedness" — diversity in nature dominates the natural order. Biodiversity provides the evidence for impermanence and species in flux. Evolutionary biologists like Dr. Bruce Bagemihl and Dr. Joan Roughgarden study this idea. Bagemihl argues for the diversity of sexual behaviour in nature in *Biological Exuberance*, and Roughgarden expanded this work to highlight the ways in which the concept of diversity extends to sex and gender in nature. What I believe is key here is to understand that what we often think is natural (stemming from nature) and normal (from culture) is much more complex and diverse than what we're taught to believe.

Culture creates the illusion that we know everything there is to know about the natural world. Culture makes us think about nature in simplistic terms: we are taught to think that "right" and "natural" behaviour is opposed to "wrong" and "unnatural" behaviour. But we can't possibly know everything about nature based on the categories devised in culture.

My non-binary identity is a hybrid of culture and nature. The term is excavated from language (culture) coming into being through human subjects, yet I believe its fluidity relates to what exists in nature. The state of being non-binary is just as "natural" and "normal" as not being non-binary. In other words, gender beyond the binary is just as natural and normal as the rigid and narrow gender system of "man" and "woman" that exists in culture around the world. It is culture that has cemented the concepts of "man" and "woman," which do not exist in nature, "male" and "female" exist in nature because scientists developed this language to make a clear distinction between the external and internal morphology (genitalia) of non-human species. Yet, scientists have made it abundantly clear that sex and gender cannot be understood as a binary.

In October 2018, 2,617 scientists around the world

(including 1,100+ biologists, 180+ geneticists, and 9 Nobel laureates) collectively signed a powerful statement in opposition to any government that intends to define gender identity, sex, or gender in terms of an immutable biological fact or according to a binary. The proposal states, "It is clear that many factors, known and unknown, mediate the complex links between identity, genes, and anatomy." Further, the scientists note that "legally defining gender as a binary condition determined at birth, based on genitalia [is] fundamentally inconsistent not only with science, but also with ethical practices, human rights, and basic dignity." Trans, non-binary, and gender-nonconforming people don't need science to validate our identities; however, when science stands on our side it reaffirms the validity of our existence.

It is culture, not nature, that bangs the drum of "normal" to make us comfortable, make us the same. But we are not all the same. And, ironically, it is in culture, by drawing from nature, that we are finding ways to resist and reclaim our truth about what is normal and natural. We need to return to nature to reclaim this space.

I exist in concordance with the wild and the free. I am most comfortable when I'm in natural environments—the earth, the trees, the birds, and the bacteria do not judge me. My hybridity stems from the nature that created me, from the cosmic dust and the micro-organisms that exist in all of us. That is the magic of humanity. We are so much more than the definitions that have been created to define and limit us. That is why non-binary offers such power and potential for us to be free when it comes to gender, sex, and even sexuality.

I want to offer non-binary as a philosophy that embraces the impermanence that governs our lives. Instead of relying on the stable, we should turn to the wild and free. Nature evolves; it doesn't remain the same, so why should we? The seasons pass and the cycles repeat with everlasting variation and adaptation. I like to think of non-binary identity and expression as being closely linked with the fluidity and impermanence that can be found in nature. The natural world never stops, it always moves forward. Why should humanity stagnate in terms of how we understand sex, gender, and sexuality? My reconnection with nature paralleled the reclamation of my identity, hidden at my very core—a combination of my body, spirit, and mind.

HOW MANY PEOPLE ABIDE by a perfect alignment of sex, gender identity, and gender expression according to normative expectations on a daily basis? Most of the people in my life who are cis men and cis women do not perfectly line up with sex and gender in a tidy way. If we truly looked, there would be very few people who, every single day of their lives, continually express and identify with the perfect alignment of masculine/male/man or feminine/female/woman. There are actually infinite variations of these combinations. This is the *real* natural way.

Ask yourself: Do you always abide by the very narrow way of presenting yourself as dictated by your gender? Do you behave and identify every day of your life in a way that perfectly lines up with the binary? Upon reflection, has your gender expression or identity shifted at all throughout your life? Some people certainly resonate with a very stable and consistent feeling about their gender, but many people don't. This doesn't mean that someone is trans, because being trans is an identity, but it can mean that a person's gender expression might fall within the realm of non-binary.

There are absolutely no rules or limits to being non-binary. It is a common misconception that non-binary is a label. Why create another label when there are enough labels? Non-binary isn't a label but rather an identity that is open and inclusive. The diversity of gender rests on an infinite spectrum rather than either-or categories. So why are non-binary people considered to be a "tiny minority" if the phenomenon of gender diversity, the very plurality and multiplicity of sex and gender, is actually more normal than we think? What will it take for people to understand that sex and gender are more complex and more personal than we have been led to believe?

Gender is what we make for ourselves, not for other people. Gender is our own. Our humanity is valid in whatever form we assume, so long as we adhere to principles of respect and compassion.

We don't have to be or look like everybody to exist; any body is valid.

THE FIXED IDENTITY CATEGORIES of "man" and "woman" will never disappear from our society. These identities are valid. Your identity won't suddenly vanish or dissipate if you open yourself up to the idea that non-binary people exist.

Each and every person has a right to identify as a man or woman, just as non-binary people have every right to be who they are.

Millennials and Gen Zers are increasingly adopting a diverse approach to gender identity and expression and sexuality. Language will always shift and evolve. We find language as we find ourselves. The evolution of our language, and the adoption of terms like *transgender* or *non-binary*, opens the space for people to be who they are.

The number of parents who give their children freedom to identify as they are is increasing. It is a common and rather harmful misconception that these parents are indoctrinating their children into an "ideology." No parent is telling their child to be trans or non-binary. They are simply allowing their children to come to terms with their own identities rather than telling them who they should be. How is this any different from parents who gender their children in line with the sex they are assigned at birth? How is it different from parents who host gender-reveal parties and begin to socialize children with a gender-designed room in blue or pink and all the toys and clothes that go along with this system of binary-based gender expression? Many parents now are simply acknowledging that gendering at birth, and enforcing the gender that follows the sex assigned at birth, can present children with a significant amount of confusion, challenges, and pain in life. Being born into a gender assignment that was presented to me as the only option opened me up to decades of suffering, so I know very well how important it is to let children be who they are. All you need to do is read my story to realize how much pain is introduced to a child's life when they are told who to be instead of by who they are.

When I was born, a gender revolution was already underway in popular culture. David Bowie, Boy George, Prince, and Grace Jones, to name just a few important figures, were all visually deconstructing the gender binary. People framed this gender deconstruction in terms of androgyny. I don't mind the word "androgynous," but I reject it when it defines a type of gender-neutrality. My gender is loud, visible, and more complex than anything the term "androgyny" can tell us. But I was born during this cultural moment when androgyny was tolerated and even celebrated on the level of expression and performance.

The gender conversion therapy with Dr. Turner that I experienced when I was eight was meant to find ways to "correct" me rather than allow me to just be me. When treating trans children today, the medical practice pays a lot of careful attention to a contextual analysis of the child, their symptoms, and their distress. Medical practitioners save lives by providing medical intervention in whatever form of gender confirmation it might take for each individual patient. It is undeniable that children who cannot access this medical care are at an increased risk of mental health problems, self-harm, and possibly even suicide. Suicide is a critical issue for trans youth and adults. Medicine is a lifesaver for some trans kids, and hormone replacement therapy has certainly helped me. But medical intervention may not hold the same answer for all trans and gender-nonconforming kids. Some trans kids need support in other forms, like therapy, supportive mechanisms in their schools, and an environment where their gender diversity is given the space to be explored, where they are celebrated and accepted. If there is one hope I have for this book, deep within the heart of opening my stories, it is this: that no child—cis, trans, non-binary, or gender-nonconforming—will ever be treated inhumanely for being their authentic self. Ever.

WRITING THIS BOOK has given me space to relive my stories. They've taken on new life. My stories are more than the traumatic reminders that have haunted me throughout my life. The void of trauma beckoned me beyond what I could remember at first. My trauma is a collection of painful memories across decades. I had to feel the memories once more in my present, at times even remembering events that were not at all accessible to me until I began to write this book. And my writing wasn't just about remembering; it was also about the need to feel again. Surviving became my priority. But opening myself to the entirety of my feelings, delving into the spirit hidden deep beneath a heart conditioned by dehumanization, was the hardest part of my journey.

Rediscovering and revisiting the feelings attached to the core of my memories was vital to my storytelling. The many years of suffering made me who I am today. Some of these stories flowed freely from the epicentre of my soul, where I kept everything hidden and safe. And some of my remembering had to come from a careful dissection of my subjectivity from an objective point of view that I found odd. Some of my stories denied that excavation; sharing them was too much to bear. I found myself crying many tears, laughing, and even feeling angry at times. The stories took shape and opened me up to reliving the past as my memories and feelings found space again, morphing into the very words and pages in this book, for once being allowed to exist as a part of my life transformed anew.

It is a deeply painful practice, indeed, to excavate suffering. I never wanted to live it all again, and it's no wonder that this exercise met with some resistance. But I had to go back to all the life-changing and life-making moments to share what I believe shaped me as a person. And then, of course, there were the intimate parts that I had kept to myself until now. This was a conscious choice. There are still some stories to tell, but I am not ready to share them yet.

Telling these stories wasn't a choice. Staying silent wasn't an option. I had to tell these stories to help encourage the humane treatment of people like me. The easy path for me would have been an existence epitomizing loneliness, wondering about the difference that I could have made with my story. I have not travelled an easy path. That isn't who I am. I followed my calling to tell my own story, made possible thanks to the generations of truth-tellers who came before me and who dared to defy the status quo.

We are warriors. We are pioneers, groundbreakers, soul-shakers, and peacemakers. We are the nails that stick up and refuse to be hammered down. We are the untamed. We are the voices that dare to say no to the same old shit and the same old stories that have been shared over and over again, voices that dare to shake the foundation of thinking that tries to separate us into one or the other, young or old, man or woman, right or left.

We are trans and non-binary, and we are human beings with stories to tell, lives to live, love in our hearts, and kindness to share. We are here to help make the world a better place simply by being ourselves.

The world needs to elevate people at the margins to share different stories than the ones that are retold over and over. When we step into a place of visibility and security, we need to reach back down and extend a hand for the sake of humanity. We need to lift each other up so that new stories can be told. We always learn from what we don't know. We can find ourselves in the stories of others, and in doing so we can make our lives, and the lives of those around us, a little better, while being true to who we are. We can create horizons of hope.

Take yourself back to when you were a child. We all have the power to work through the cultural conditioning if we want to. I got so tired of being the Josh that was created for me. I reclaimed my identity. I reclaimed little Joshua, and the path wasn't simple. I was once a young and free spirit before the mess of the binary entered my life. I found myself again. I always knew that something wasn't quite right when I reached adulthood. So I embarked on a path of wondering myself through my pain and suffering. Curiosity guided my quest back to myself. Who I was, am, will be. It is never too late to feel *connected* with who we are, *to be* who we are, to be who *you* are.

I am Joshua M. Ferguson. I am non-binary. With these words, these stories, finally, my story can have its true beginning.

Glossary

I know that the language associated with the discussion of trans lives can be an obstacle, and that many people have questions about correct terminology. People often express a fear about using the wrong pronouns, or not understanding the importance of pronouns for trans people. Here's a useful primer for the language used in this book.

GENDER is an especially complicated term because its very definition changes depending on the time and place in which it is used. Gender is about socially constructed norms, specific to a time and place; the concept exists relative to cultural and historical specificity. Because the definition of gender is based on language and cultural practice, it is different around the world. Nonetheless, gender is also used in a similar way to understand identity, particularly in the West and in Western-colonized cultures, where Euro-centric value systems destroyed the diverse cultural understandings of sex and gender that existed prior to colonization.

Many cultures around the world believe gender to be exclusively male or female. Most societies tend to assume that gender comes naturally from sex, and that they are the same. At the very least, there is a general understanding that a relationship exists between the two terms. Gender is a complex, multilayered, ideologically saturated concept that escapes a static and clear definition. It is a combination of things, open to how our understanding shifts, similar to the openness of the term *non-binary*. And it can be a vital part of understanding who we are as human beings and how we relate to one another.

SEX is typically defined by external and internal morphology (genitalia) and chromosomal makeup (xx, xy, xxy, and so on). The Western imperative to conflate sex and gender has resulted in the interchangeable use of these terms. Some people think that making a clear distinction between the terms is important; however, it is now increasingly common for trans people, including non-binary people, to understand that there is no real distinction between sex and gender when it comes to our identities. I identify both my gender and my sex as non-binary. Consequently, we often think of *sex* to mean only male or female and the attached gendered terms of *man* and *woman*, with nothing beyond the two possible options, completely excluding intersex people.

GENDER IDENTITY is how we perceive our sense of self in relation to gender. Gender identities are diverse, so one might identify as male, female, man, woman, intersex, non-binary, or none, all, or even some of the above. Gender identity is a self-determined subjective relationship we have with our gender, our gender expression, and our sexed body.

GENDER EXPRESSION relates to our mannerisms and behaviour, and the way we style our body to present and express our gender identity. Gender expression can be fluid or relatively static. For most people, gender expression is fluid, meaning that the way we express our gender can change greatly from, for example, childhood to adolescence to adulthood or even from day to day, or year to year. Gender expression does not have to correlate with gender identity in a normative sense. For example, a non-binary person can have a very feminine or masculine gender expression instead of a more androgynous presentation. The latter expression is typically expected for non-binary people, but it isn't always our reality. Gender expression exists on a spectrum rather than the masculine vs. feminine binary that we are caught up with in language. I would argue that there are infinite gender expressions, although we tend to think about our expression in a singular way. A person's gender expression does not automatically define their gender identity. These are two different things. Gender identity and gender expression are not synonymous, and they can simultaneously contribute to the notion of gender.

BINARY is a term used to define the polar opposites that are pervasive in a Western way of structuring language and thought about gender: woman/man, feminine/masculine, weak/strong, and so on. One side of the binary is usually implied to be superior and the other inferior, a structure that has supported patriarchy, a system in which cis men are afforded privileges that cis women are not. The binaries of sex, gender, and sexuality are so entrenched in our language and the way we think about one another that it is difficult to imagine any reality outside of these binaries, but realizing that life and the world cannot be understood exclusively within a binary makes for a diverse and colourful existence. We just have to think about it to realize the non-binary parts of our lives.

NON-BINARY is not the opposite of *binary*. *Non-binary* is a rather new term used to describe sex and/or gender identity that is neither exclusively one nor the other of male and female, or neither male/man nor female/woman. Non-binary is an anti-category in the sense that it defies a stable definition. Since gender identity is self-determined, it is important to realize that *non-binary* is an inclusive term for an infinite variation of sexes, gender identities, and gender expressions. *Non-binary* has swiftly become the umbrella term for identities that are neither men nor women, but some non-binary people can identify as non-binary trans women or non-binary trans men.

TRANSGENDER literally means "across genders" and refers to someone whose sexed body and gender identity do not conform to societal expectations. *Transgender* is still used as an umbrella term for trans people: trans men, trans women, non-binary people, and gender-nonconforming people. However, its use in the vernacular, especially in the media and popular culture, mostly refers to trans men and trans women: trans people who often transition to match the gender identity that they are born with and that might conflict with their sex assignment at birth.

CIS and **CISGENDER** refer to people who are on the "same side" of their assigned sex at birth and their gender identity. The sex and gender identity of cis people line up in terms of cultural expectations.

TRANS/TRANS PEOPLE has become an umbrella term for the transgender community.

SEXUALITY is related to how we identify our sexual expression, attraction, and desire. Sexualities can be static for one's entire life, or sexuality can change throughout life. Common sexual identities include, but are not limited to: heterosexual, lesbian, gay, bisexual, queer, asexual, and pansexual. Sexuality is not entirely dependent on gender identity and it shouldn't be confused with sex.

PRONOUNS are used to refer to people's gender identity in language. The two common pronoun groups in the English language are she/her/hers and he/him/his. There are several gender-neutral pronouns, but they/them/their is the most prevalent pronoun group for non-binary people.

Timeline of Non-Binary Legal Recognition Around the World

The timeline that follows illustrates the undeniable momentum for non-binary legal recognition globally. Although non-binary is not always named explicitly in these policies and laws, I'm using it as a catch-all phrase for any international policy or law that aims to include people who are neither male nor female, men nor women. There could be dates and changes in countries that are not included in this timeline, but it does aim to be comprehensive in its representation of the reality of change around the world for non-binary people.

DECEMBER 27, 2007 (NEPAL): Nepal is the first country in the world to recognize people who are neither male or female. The Supreme Court of Nepal establishes a "third gender" category on this date.

SEPTEMBER 15, 2011 (AUSTRALIA): Australia provides a third gender option "X" for passports.

DECEMBER 5, 2012 (NEW ZEALAND): The country introduces a third gender option, "X (indeterminate/unspecified)," on passports.

APRIL 15, 2014 (INDIA): The Supreme Court of India legally recognizes a third gender (typically called *hijra*) classification, citing it as a human rights issue.

MARCH 21, 2014 (AUSTRALIA): The country's Australian Capital Territory introduces an "X" option for birth certificates.

JULY 17, 2015 (NEW ZEALAND): Statistics New Zealand introduces a gender diverse category, making it the first country in the world with this type of inclusion for statistical purposes.

JUNE 2016 (UNITED STATES): Jamie Shupe wins a court challenge in Oregon to become the first legally recognized nonbinary person in the country.

JUNE 2016 (CANADA): Ontario becomes the first province in the country to offer health cards that no longer display sex or gender.

SEPTEMBER 2016 (UNITED STATES): Sara Kelly Keenan wins a court challenge in California to become the second person in the country to be legally recognized as non-binary.

DECEMBER 2016 (UNITED STATES): Keenan then becomes the first person in the United States with an intersex birth certificate.

JANUARY 2017 (CANADA): Christin Milloy, along with barbara findlay (who uses lowercase letters) and the Gender Free ID Coalition, win a court case that makes it possible for Canadians to identify as non-binary on Employment and Social Development Canada documentation.

FEBRUARY 2017 (UNITED STATES): Star Hagen-Esquerra of California becomes the first legally recognized non-binary minor in the country.

MARCH 2017 (UNITED STATES): Sara Kelly Keenan and fellow non-binary advocates work with the State Assembly's senators in California to introduce Bill SB 179. Governor Jerry Brown is expected to sign this bill into law in the fall of 2017, which would make California the first district in North America to provide a non-binary option on birth certificates. This bill would legally recognize non-binary gender identity on all forms of identification, including birth certificates and driver's licences. And the bill would remove two requirements necessary for a gender change on documentation: providing a physician's statement, and appearing in person in court. Finally, the bill includes a provision to make it easier for minors to apply for gender changes on their birth certificates.

MARCH 2017 (CANADA): The Province of Ontario's "X" option on driver's licences becomes available.

APRIL 2017 (CANADA): Gemma Hickey becomes the first person in Canada to publicly apply for a non-binary birth certificate.

MAY 2017 (CANADA): Prime Minister Justin Trudeau and Minister of Justice and Attorney General Jody Wilson-Raybould announce that the Canadian government is working with Passport Canada to implement an "X" option on Canadian passports.

MAY 2017 (CANADA): Joshua M. Ferguson publicly applies for a non-binary birth certificate in Ontario.

JUNE 2017 (UNITED STATES): In the District of Columbia, Nic Sakurai becomes the first person in the country to receive a non-binary driver's licence. The law also implements a self-attestation form instead of a physician's letter for a change of gender. The ability to self-attest to one's gender identity removes barriers that many people face to access ID changes.

JUNE 2017 (UNITED STATES): Oregon becomes the first state to offer an "X" option on driver's licences.

JUNE 2017 (CANADA): Gemma Hickey takes the Province of Newfoundland and Labrador to the provincial Supreme Court over the denial of their non-binary birth certificate application. A court date is set for late July 2017.

JUNE 2017 (CANADA): Bill C-16 becomes law in Canada. This legislation amends the Canadian Human Rights Act to include gender identity and gender expression as protected grounds. It also amends the Criminal Code to extend protection against Hate Propaganda set out in the Act for gender identity and gender expression.

JUNE 2017 (CANADA): A baby is issued a health card with a "U" designation, meaning "sex unassigned" (believed to be first in the world). This action is led by the baby's parent Kori Doty, who is represented by barbara findlay with the Gender Free ID Coalition. The Province of British Columbia still refuses to issue a birth certificate without a sex marker.

JULY 2017 (CANADA): The Northwest Territories becomes the first jurisdiction in Canada to implement a policy for non-binary birth certificates.

AUGUST 2017 (CANADA): Joshua M. Ferguson files a human rights complaint against the Province of Ontario for their non-binary birth certificate.

AUGUST 2017 (CANADA): Canada's federal government sets a precedent by legally recognizing non-binary people for the first time with its plan for Canadian passports. The Ministry of Immigration and Refugee Services announces an interim policy to allow non-binary people to receive an observation on their passport with an "X" marker until they can implement a system change to provide the full sex marker of "X."

SEPTEMBER 2017 (UNITED STATES): California makes history for non-binary legal recognition by passing comprehensive legislation to recognize non-binary people on all forms of identification, removing the requirement for a physician's letter for a change of sex designation, and including protection for non-binary people under the law.

SEPTEMBER 2017 (CANADA): The Province of Newfoundland and Labrador implements a policy for non-binary birth certificates and announces legislation to legally recognize non-binary people on driver's licences.

OCTOBER 2017 (CANADA): Joshua M. Ferguson files a human rights complaint against the Province of British Columbia for their non-binary short-form designation on their combined health card and driver's licence.

NOVEMBER 2017 (CANADA): Gemma Hickey receives their non-binary birth certificate in Newfoundland and Labrador.

JANUARY 2018 (UNITED STATES): Washington State becomes the fourth jurisdiction in the nation to make non-binary birth certificates and driver's licences available to residents, while several other states consider non-binary gender markers on state-issued ID. This new policy means that the entire west coast of the country now offers a non-binary gender marker on forms of government-issued identification. There are several states—New York, New Jersey, Maryland, and Massachusetts—that have pending legislation to implement non-binary options on government-issued ID.

FEBRUARY 2018 (GREECE): Jason Antigone Dane becomes the first person in the country to be given the option to identify as a non-binary person on their ID after a court ruled in their favour.

MAY 7, 2018 (CANADA): Joshua M. Ferguson is issued Ontario's first non-binary birth certificate after successfully resolving their human rights complaint with the province. Ontario becomes the first jurisdiction in the world to offer four options for birth certificates: M, F, X, or no gender marker.

MAY 25, 2018 (CANADA): A court ruling in Saskatchewan makes it the first jurisdiction in Canada to rule that citizens, even minors, must have an option to apply to have their gender marker removed from birth certificates.

MAY 28, 2018 (NETHERLANDS): A Dutch court rules that "third gender" should be legally recognized.

JUNE 8, 2018 (CANADA): Alberta Premier Rachel Notley announces a new policy to recognize non-binary people on birth certificates and driver's licences with a "gender-inclusive" "X" marker.

JUNE 11, 2018 (UNITED STATES): The State of Maine announces a policy for non-binary driver's licences and other forms of identification.

JUNE 15, 2018 (AUSTRIA): The Austrian Constitutional Court confirms that Article 8 of the European Convention on

Human Rights guarantees recognition of gender identity beyond the binary of male and female. There is an option to apply for an "empty" entry for sex on documents but no name has been decided upon (*divers, inter, offen* being considered).

AUGUST 15, 2018 (GERMANY): Although Germany was the first country in Europe to allow for a blank entry on birth certificates for intersex-born children, it's not until this date, more than six months after the nation's highest court ruled in favour of an intersex individual to be legally recognized, that Germany's cabinet approves third gender recognition on official records, allowing people to identify as "diverse."

SEPTEMBER 12, 2018 (UNITED STATES): New York City announces a new city-wide policy for non-binary birth certificates that will be available beginning January 1, 2019.

SEPTEMBER 19, 2018 (CANADA): Nova Scotia implements a policy for "X" designations on birth certificates.

OCTOBER 1, 2018 (UNITED STATES): Minnesota implements a policy for "X" designations on driver's licences beginning on this date.

OCTOBER 19, 2018 (THE NETHERLANDS): The first Dutch passport with an "X" designation is issued to Leonne Zeegers after they win a lawsuit. The Hague reports that "about 4 percent of the Dutch public identifies as neither male nor female."

NOVEMBER 2, 2018 (CANADA): British Columbia introduces new policy for "X" designations on all forms of government-issued identification, including driver's licences, care cards, and birth certificates.

NOVEMBER 8, 2018 (UNITED STATES): Colorado implements a policy for "X" designations on driver's licences.

NOVEMBER 30, 2018 (CANADA): Prince Edward Island becomes the first province to offer four gender designations on driver's licences: M, F, X, and blank.

APPENDIX III

LGBTQ Support Resources

CANADA

TRANS LIFELINE | 1-877-330-6366
Trans Lifeline is a national trans-led organization dedicated to improving the quality of trans lives by responding to the critical needs of the community with direct service, material support, advocacy, and education. The purpose of Trans Lifeline is to fight the epidemic of trans suicide and improve overall life-outcomes of trans people by facilitating justice-oriented, collective community aid.

LGBT YOUTH LINE | 1-800-268-9688 / Text 1-647-694-4275
The LGBT Youth Line is a toll-free Ontario-wide peer-support phone line for lesbian, gay bisexual, transgender, transsexual, two-spirited, queer, and questioning young people.

KIDS HELP PHONE

1-800-668-6868 / Text CONNECT to 686868

Kids Help Phone is Canada's only 24/7, national support service, offering professional counselling, information and referrals, and volunteer-led, text-based support to young people in both English and French.

INTERLIGNE (French and English service) | 1-888-505-1010

Interligne est un centre de première ligne en matière d'aide et de renseignements à l'intention des personnes concernées par la diversité sexuelle et la pluralité des genres.

CANADIAN PARENTS OF TRANS KIDS

parentsoftranskids@gmail.com

Canadian Parents of Trans Kids is a support group for parents of gender diverse children, youth, and adults. Parents canadiens d'enfants trans est un groupe d'entraide pour les parents/les gardiens d'enfants, de jeunes, et d'adultes de divers genres.

PFLAG CANADa | 1-888-530-6777

PFLAG Canada is a national charitable organization, founded by parents who wished to help themselves and their family members understand and accept their LGBTQ+ children.

UNITED STATES

TRANS LIFELINE | 1-877-565-8860

Trans Lifeline is a national trans-led organization dedicated to improving the quality of trans lives by responding to the critical needs of the community with direct service, material support, advocacy, and education. The purpose of Trans Lifeline is to fight the epidemic of trans suicide and improve overall life-outcomes of trans people by facilitating justice-oriented, collective community aid.

TREVOR PROJECT | 1-866-488-7386 / Text START to 678678

Founded in 1998 by the creators of the Academy Award–winning short film *Trevor,* The Trevor Project is the leading national organization providing crisis intervention and suicide prevention services to lesbian, gay, bisexual, transgender, and questioning (LGBTQ) young people ages 13–24.

PFLAG NATIONAL | 1-202-467-8180

Uniting people who are lesbian, gay, bisexual, transgender, and queer (LGBTQ) with families, friends, and allies, PFLAG is committed to advancing equality through its mission of support, education, and advocacy.

ACKNOWLEDGEMENTS

WRITING *ME, MYSELF, THEY* wouldn't have been possible without the people acknowledged in these pages. I am grateful for the family, friends, and teachers who guided me, the Amazons who supported and protected me, and the champions who never left my side and who continue to come into my life. I sincerely apologize if I have missed anyone in these pages. Committing my gratitude to paper is a heavy and important task, and one that I decided not to distill but to give space for because *connection is everything.*

My teachers, first and foremost.

Dr. Wendy Gay Pearson. Thank you for being the formative force that gave me the tools to think through my trauma and to reconnect with my identity. I will always be grateful to you for your time and your warmth of spirit, and for seeing me. I began to find my words with your wisdom.

Dr. Susan Knabe, for understanding my need for guidance, for introducing me to your beautiful partner, and for your kind lessons and empathy. Thank you for your friendship.

Mr. Barry Roantree, for being one of the first teachers to believe in me. Perhaps the first. Wherever your spirit is now, I hope that my work honours the legacy that you imparted as a teacher at H. H. Langford. Thank you.

Dr. Sharalyn Orbaugh, for becoming my mentor and champion at UBC. Your unwavering support encouraged me to reach beyond the expectations I had set for myself. It was truly an honour to be your student, and it's an honour to now be your friend.

Dr. Chika Kinoshita, for recognizing the reason behind my passion for Japanese culture and helping me articulate this powerful connection in my academic work. *Shin'ai naru* Dr. Kinoshita, *domo arigato gozaimasu*.

Dr. Barb Bruce, for the fact that you are a gift to your students. You brought to light my love for film, a romance that I can recall from childhood. Thank you for your belief in me, and for your guidance.

Dr. Ernest Mathijs, for your guidance and support during a time of academic expansion towards an uncertain yet exciting future at UBC.

Dr. Treena Orchard, for the honest conversations, love, support, and encouragement.

Dr. Leonora A. Angeles, for your kindness, your warm generosity of heart, and your passion.

Dr. Gillian Creese, for your support of my doctoral work. I will always be thankful.

Dr. Janina Falkowska, for your curiosity, your unique perspective and your lessons.

Hanako Arai: wherever you are now, you opened my world and my eyes, and I am eternally grateful. *Shin'ai naru Hanako-san, domo arigato gozaimasu.*

Thank you also to my other teachers and mentors along the way: Dr. Paul Coates, Dr. Susan Cox, Dr. Chris Shelley, Dr. Brian McIlroy, Dr. Erin Baines, Dr. Bonnie MacLachlan, Mrs. Broomhead, Mr. Hanna, Dr. Joshua Mostow, Susie Ralph, Al Rankin, and Wynn Archibald.

The magic shared by people through a handshake, their words, their music, their writing, their work, their art: Princess Diana, Carrie Fisher, Madonna, Cyndi Lauper, the creator of *Jem* (Hasbro and Christy Marx), Rosie O'Donnell, Ellen DeGeneres, Alanis Morrissette, Courtney Love, Tori Amos, Marlene Dietrich, Tilda Swinton, Angelina Jolie, Pedro Almodóvar, Kate Bornstein, Jack Halberstam, Judith Butler, and Leslie Feinberg.

For the childhood friendships that we shared, Laura Bredahl, Robert Hornsby, and Kristin Korderas. Thank you for being my friends when many found me weird and "different."

Eve Fiorillo, for your incredible force. Thank you for showing me that being true to oneself matters more than anything else.

My Amazons, Chantel, Becky, Jenna, and Amanda, for supporting and protecting me when I decided to face my fear in Napanee. I'll always hold each of you close to my heart.

Mel, Anjeet, Emily, Greg, Pete — our friendships created at Western left a legacy. I'm so proud of what we accomplished together.

Laura McPhie, for being the heart of our collective at Western after we met, gazing up at the stars together. Your constant belief in me, your encouragement, and your support are so appreciated. I love you. You have my thanks.

My Amazons at UBC, Kat Fobear and Rahela Nayebzadah, for seeing me at a pivotal time before coming out as trans and continuing to be there.

My angel, my champion, Rosemarie A. Delgado, for your kindness has changed my life. You have made so much possible for me. I love you. *Maraming salamat.*

Jules Arita Koostachin, for your friendship is a true gift. Jake, Asivak, Mahiigan, Tapwewin, and Pawaken as well. Thank you for trusting me, for your love, and for opening your family to me. *Chi-miigwech.*

Thank you to the friends who have come into my life in beautiful and unexpected ways, and who have supported me: "Gabriel," Quinn Nelson, Odessa Bennett, Elizabeth Berry, Ken Turcotte, Joy Choco, Cheri DiNovo, Kathleen Monk, Lana Parrilla, Laura Mennell, Alexa Davalos, Florence Ashley, Sam K. MacKinnon, Lauren Abrams, Gemma M. Hickey, and A.J. Lowik. I'm grateful for your many gifts, love, and support.

Thank you to my creative collaborators who have contributed to my path as a filmmaker. There are so many that I could name here, and I appreciate each and every person who has been both cast and crew on my films.

Ameko Eks Mass Carroll, for being so inspirational, so kind, and so generous with your spirit.

Noriko, *domo arigato gozaimasu* for the tea, the laughs, your kind spirit, and your open heart.

Frances Mahon (fellow Amazon), Mika Imai, and Michelle Thomarat: thank you for your time, energy, and commitment to upholding trans human rights.

Allison Cohen, for *believing* in me. This book wouldn't have been possible with you. Thank you for appreciating my voice and my writing.

Joe Veltre and the Gersh Agency, for your assistance and your commitment to supporting my work. You have my thanks.

Sarah MacLachlan, Janie Yoon, Laura Chapnick, Carolyn McNeillie, Karen Brochu, Cindy Ma, Holley Corfield, Joshua Greenspon, and the many members of House of Anansi's staff that have had a hand in bringing my book to life and getting it into the hands of readers. Thank you, House of Anansi, for investing in emerging Canadian authors; thank you for investing in me.

Maria Golikova, for your very kind heart and careful editorial attention to my story. Thank you. And many thanks to copyeditor Catherine Marjoribanks and proofreader Tara Tovell.

Laura Meyer, for our many lovely conversations and your encouragement, strategizing, and constant support. Thank you.

Brendan Meadows, for coming along with me for part of this journey, for the spells we summoned together in the studio, gathering forth the cover photograph you captured for this book. Thank you to the rest of the team at our photoshoot: stylist goddess Odessa Bennett, makeup artist Davina Faye, hair designer Florencia Cepeda, and photography assistants Maria C. Turner and Kitt Woodland.

Thank you also to makeup artist Lisa Love for my author-photo look.

Douglas Richmond. Where do I begin when your wisdom, insight, and support exist in every single line on every single page of this book? Thank you for making sure that my voice was never compromised by layers of editing. Thank you for our conversations, for your impassioned belief in my story, and for taking a chance on a new writer. I feel such gratitude for your investment in me. It's been a special process working with you to bring to life memories I had long forgotten. Thank you for your steady and constant guidance.

Thank you to my family.

Mutti and Omi. Even though I only knew both of you for a short time, your energy and love will remain with me forever. I look at my incredible husband and see both of you within him and around him. Thank you for accepting me, for the communication we shared in many forms. May you both be at peace, always, angels with angels.

The Hess family in Engelberg. Thank you for welcoming me into your family and opening your hearts to me.

Ed, Laurie, Kristina, Uncle Joe and Aunt Leslie, Emma, Morgan, Halie, Uncle Mike, Uncle Ralphie, Poppa Ralph, Laura: thank you to my family for supporting and loving me.

My grandparents, for your love and support even though most of your spirits have moved on. Thank you to my single-surviving grandparent, my Pop Stuart, for loving me and seeing me.

My Nan Thelma, for you are my angel. Always there two steps behind me, with me. You saw me, listened to me.

We learned from one another, and I hope my story has honoured you. You were one of my best friends. I'll always carry you with me and will love you always.

My Nan Lois, for you are my muse. I can feel you with me. I can still hear your voice. I can still see the illuminating force that surrounded you when you walked into a space. I will love you always. I will cherish the connection we shared, and I will make you proud.

My brother James, for loving me and supporting me. You've always made me feel less like an outcast by seeing me for who I am. Thank you for travelling with me, reviewing my early academic work, and all the laughter and lessons we've shared together.

My brother Adam, for loving me and supporting me. You've always made me feel protected by being there. Thank you for believing in me, for telling me not to give a shit if other people don't value me, and for entertaining the many plays and skits I used to direct with you and James when we were kids.

Mom and Dad, for being parents that all trans people would be fortunate to have. I am blessed by your steadfast belief in allowing me to be who I am despite the conflicting messages both of you were receiving from sources outside of our family. Thank you for showing me how to care for nature and for human beings. I hope to continue to make you proud of me for years to come. I love you both, forever.

Florian, *for everything*. You have made it all possible. Your light, your love, your heart, your smile, and your embrace have been powerful remedies for the dehumanization and pain written in this book. Without your love, I wouldn't have been able to come home to myself. Together forever, my love, my star. You had me at "hello, you." You will always have my deepest and eternal thanks. This book is for *you*.

JOSHUA M. FERGUSON (PH.D.) is a non-binary trans (they/them) writer, filmmaker, advocate, and alchemist. In 2018, they became the first person to receive a non-binary birth certificate with an "X" designation in their home province of Ontario, and their advocacy on behalf of non-binary trans people has contributed to government reform in Canada. With their production company, Turbid Lake Pictures, Ferguson's filmmaking work includes the award-winning *Whispers of Life*; *Limina*, which was shown at festivals around the world and praised for its trans inclusivity; and the love story *Henry's Heart*. Their writing and advocacy efforts have been featured in international publications including the *Toronto Star*, the *Guardian*, NBC News, *HuffPost*, *VICE*, *BuzzFeed*, *Teen Vogue*, and *OUT Magazine*. Ferguson lives in Vancouver, British Columbia, with their partner Florian. *Me, Myself, They* is their first book.

@joshuamferguson